"This series is a tremendous resource for those w understanding of how the gospel is woven thro pastors and scholars doing gospel business from a. logical feast preparing God's people to apply the entire Bible to all of life with heart and mind wholly committed to Christ's priorities."

BRYAN CHAPELL, President Emeritus, Covenant Theological Seminary; Senior Pastor, Grace Presbyterian Church, Peoria, Illinois

"Mark Twain may have smiled when he wrote to a friend, 'I didn't have time to write you a short letter, so I wrote you a long letter.' But the truth of Twain's remark remains serious and universal, because well-reasoned, compact writing requires extra time and extra hard work. And this is what we have in the Crossway Bible study series *Knowing the Bible*. The skilled authors and notable editors provide the contours of each book of the Bible as well as the grand theological themes that bind them together as one Book. Here, in a 12-week format, are carefully wrought studies that will ignite the mind and the heart."

R. KENT HUGHES, Visiting Professor of Practical Theology, Westminster Theological Seminary

"*Knowing the Bible* brings together a gifted team of Bible teachers to produce a high-quality series of study guides. The coordinated focus of these materials is unique: biblical content, provocative questions, systematic theology, practical application, and the gospel story of God's grace presented all the way through Scripture."

PHILIP G. RYKEN, President, Wheaton College

"These *Knowing the Bible* volumes provide a significant and very welcome variation on the general run of inductive Bible studies. This series provides substantial instruction, as well as teaching through the very questions that are asked. *Knowing the Bible* then goes even further by showing how any given text links with the gospel, the whole Bible, and the formation of theology. I heartily endorse this orientation of individual books to the whole Bible and the gospel, and I applaud the demonstration that sound theology was not something invented later by Christians, but is right there in the pages of Scripture."

GRAEME L. GOLDSWORTHY, former lecturer, Moore Theological College; author, *According to Plan, Gospel and Kingdom, The Gospel in Revelation,* and *Gospel and Wisdom*

"What a gift to earnest, Bible-loving, Bible-searching believers! The organization and structure of the Bible study format presented through the *Knowing the Bible* series is so well conceived. Students of the Word are led to understand the content of passages through perceptive, guided questions, and they are given rich insights and application all along the way in the brief but illuminating sections that conclude each study. What potential growth in depth and breadth of understanding these studies offer! One can only pray that vast numbers of believers will discover more of God and the beauty of his Word through these rich studies."

BRUCE A. WARE, Professor of Christian Theology, The Southern Baptist Theological Seminary

KNOWING THE BIBLE

J. I. Packer, Theological Editor
Dane C. Ortlund, Series Editor
Lane T. Dennis, Executive Editor

•   •   •   •   •   •

Genesis	Psalms	Jonah, Micah, and Nahum	Ephesians
Exodus	Proverbs	Haggai, Zechariah, and Malachi	Philippians
Leviticus	Ecclesiastes		Colossians and Philemon
Numbers	Song of Solomon	Matthew	1–2 Thessalonians
Deuteronomy	Isaiah	Mark	1–2 Timothy and Titus
Joshua	Jeremiah	Luke	Hebrews
Judges	Lamentations, Habakkuk, and Zephaniah	John	James
Ruth and Esther		Acts	1–2 Peter and Jude
1–2 Samuel	Ezekiel	Romans	1–3 John
1–2 Kings	Daniel	1 Corinthians	Revelation
1–2 Chronicles	Hosea	2 Corinthians	
Ezra and Nehemiah	Joel, Amos, and Obadiah	Galatians	
Job			

•   •   •   •   •   •

J. I. PACKER is Board of Governors' Professor of Theology at Regent College (Vancouver, BC). Dr. Packer earned his DPhil at the University of Oxford. He is known and loved worldwide as the author of the best-selling book *Knowing God*, as well as many other titles on theology and the Christian life. He serves as the General Editor of the ESV Bible and as the Theological Editor for the *ESV Study Bible*.

LANE T. DENNIS is President of Crossway, a not-for-profit publishing ministry. Dr. Dennis earned his PhD from Northwestern University. He is Chair of the ESV Bible Translation Oversight Committee and Executive Editor of the *ESV Study Bible*.

DANE C. ORTLUND is Executive Vice President of Bible Publishing and Bible Publisher at Crossway. He is a graduate of Covenant Theological Seminary (MDiv, ThM) and Wheaton College (BA, PhD). Dr. Ortlund has authored several books and scholarly articles in the areas of Bible, theology, and Christian living.

LAMENTATIONS, HABAKKUK, AND ZEPHANIAH

A 12-WEEK STUDY

Camden M. Bucey

∷ CROSSWAY®

WHEATON, ILLINOIS

Knowing the Bible: Lamentations, Habakkuk, and Zephaniah, A 12-Week Study

Copyright © 2018 by Crossway

Published by Crossway
    1300 Crescent Street
    Wheaton, Illinois 60187

Cover design: Simplicated Studio

First printing 2018

Printed in the United States of America

Trade paperback ISBN: 978-1-4335-5741-5
EPub ISBN: 978-1-4335-5744-6
PDF ISBN: 978-1-4335-5742-2
Mobipocket ISBN: 978-1-4335-5743-9

Crossway is a publishing ministry of Good News Publishers.

VP		28	27	26	25	24	23	22	21	20	19	18
15	14	13	12	11	10	9	8	7	6	5	4	3	2	1

TABLE OF CONTENTS

SERIES PREFACE

KNOWING THE BIBLE, as the series title indicates, was created to help readers know and understand the meaning, the message, and the God of the Bible. Each volume in the series consists of 12 units that progressively take the reader through a clear, concise study of one or more books of the Bible. In this way, any given volume can fruitfully be used in a 12-week format either in group study, such as in a church-based context, or in individual study. Of course, these 12 studies could be completed in fewer or more than 12 weeks, as convenient, depending on the context in which they are used.

Each study unit gives an overview of the text at hand before digging into it with a series of questions for reflection or discussion. The unit then concludes by highlighting the gospel of grace in each passage ("Gospel Glimpses"), identifying whole-Bible themes that occur in the passage ("Whole-Bible Connections"), and pinpointing Christian doctrines that are affirmed in the passage ("Theological Soundings").

The final component to each unit is a section for reflecting on personal and practical implications from the passage at hand. The layout provides space for recording responses to the questions proposed, and we think readers need to do this to get the full benefit of the exercise. The series also includes definitions of key words. These definitions are indicated by a note number in the text and are found at the end of each chapter.

Lastly, to help understand the Bible in this deeper way, we urge readers to use the ESV Bible and the *ESV Study Bible*, which are available in various print and digital formats, including online editions at esv.org. The *Knowing the Bible* series is also available online.

May the Lord greatly bless your study as you seek to know him through knowing his Word.

J. I. Packer
Lane T. Dennis

Week 1: Overview of Lamentations, Habakkuk, and Zephaniah

▲

Getting Acquainted

Lamentations, Habakkuk, and Zephaniah are rich with God's truths concerning our sin and need of redemption as well as God's love for us in the Savior, Jesus Christ. The prophecies contained in these books are far removed from our historical context, but they are much needed and are applicable to our contemporary issues. While Lamentations, Habakkuk, and Zephaniah speak within particular contexts, they also transcend those contexts to address God's people in all ages. The apostle Paul declares, "All Scripture is breathed out by God and profitable for teaching, for reproof, for correction, and for training in righteousness, that the man of God may be complete, equipped for every good work" (2 Tim. 3:16–17). This is true for the well-worn portions of our Bibles as well as for the shorter books of the Old Testament that receive much less attention. Together, Lamentations, Habakkuk, and Zephaniah express the pain and suffering of God's people as they live in a fallen world. The people suffer at the hands of their enemies, who have been sent by the Lord himself. But the people are not without hope, and this suffering is not meaningless, because God uses this form of <u>fatherly discipline</u> to sanctify and restore his people.

(For further background, see the *ESV Study Bible*, pages 1585–1588, 1847–1848, and 1857–1859; available online at www.esv.org.)

> ### Placing Lamentations, Habakkuk, and Zephaniah in the Larger Story

The title of Lamentations in the Hebrew Bible is a Hebrew word translated "How," which is the first word of Lamentations and begins chapters 2 and 4 as well. This term is an exclamation of how much Jerusalem has suffered. Although this suffering is overwhelming, the author pours out his heart beautifully. The book of Lamentations is structured in five poems, which align with the five chapters in our English Bible. The first four poems are acrostics; that is, each new line begins with the next letter in the Hebrew alphabet. The author of the book is not specifically identified, yet some believe him to be the prophet Jeremiah, who "uttered a lament for Josiah" (2 Chron. 35:25). Regardless of who put the lament to the scroll, the voice is corporate and expresses the suffering of the people. Lamentations is a eulogy for the death of the kingdom of Judah, which has been taken away into exile. The situation is stark and bleak, yet there is hope in God, whose mercies are new every morning. He is the faithful and compassionate one who forgets not his people—even as they suffer justly for what they have done.

Habakkuk shares a struggle that many Christians throughout the ages have experienced: If God is loving and in control, why are the wicked so successful? While Habakkuk demonstrates an understanding of God's attributes, he still struggles to understand how God can use the wicked to accomplish his divine purpose. God's ways are mysterious, and the realization of Habakkuk's prophecy will mean suffering for the people of God, yet "the righteous shall live by his faith" (2:4). God's people must look not to themselves but to another—to Jesus Christ. Their confidence does not rest in their own strength, nor in their ability to comprehend everything. It rests instead in the Lord, who is at work on behalf of his covenant people even before they cry out to him.

Zephaniah experiences the same suffering as Habakkuk. However, Zephaniah offers a theological perspective distinct from his contemporary. The prophet speaks of the "day of the LORD," in which the Lord will put an end to corruption and wickedness. This has been the longing of God's people throughout the ages. The faithful have always cried out to the Lord for help in the face of evil and injustice. But Zephaniah raises a deeper issue as he turns his attention inward. What happens when *God's people* are the wicked ones? Judgment must begin in the house of the Lord (1 Pet. 4:17). All manner of injustice has spread throughout the nation of Judah, and before God's people can enter their everlasting rest, they too must be sanctified. Zephaniah demonstrates how God's wrath pertains to his relationship with the world generally and with his people specifically. The Lord visits his people in judgment many times in history, but the great and final "day of the LORD" will come when Christ returns on the last day. God calls his people to seek him (Zeph. 2:3) so that they might escape the wrath to come.

Key Verses

"The steadfast love of the LORD never ceases; his mercies never come to an end; they are new every morning; great is your faithfulness. 'The LORD is my portion,' says my soul, 'therefore I will hope in him.'" (Lam. 3:22–24)

". . . the righteous shall live by his faith." (Hab. 2:4)

"The LORD has taken away the judgments against you; he has cleared away your enemies. The King of Israel, the LORD, is in your midst; you shall never again fear evil." (Zeph. 3:15)

Date and Historical Background

Lamentations is the cry of God's people, who have experienced devastation. The book was most likely written just after Jerusalem fell to the Babylonians in 587 BC. The author writes from personal experience and describes many horrific things in detail. While there is no precise date of composition within the book, it implies that temple worship, which would begin again in the time of Haggai and Zechariah between 520 and 516 BC, had temporarily ceased. Moreover, Lamentations conveys the sense of recent suffering. The people bear an open wound that has not yet begun to heal. Therefore, it was likely written closer to 587 BC than to 516.

Habakkuk was likely written several years prior to Lamentations, somewhere between 640 and 609 BC. The prophet delivered the word of the Lord just before the fall of Assyria. He prophesied that God would use Babylon ("the Chaldeans") to punish Judah, just as he had used Assyria to punish Israel in 722 (Hab. 1:6). This prophecy was fulfilled in 587 and was the occasion for the suffering described in Lamentations. It does not appear that the Babylonians were at the city gates at the time of the composition of Habakkuk. Nonetheless, Habakkuk was aware of the imminent threat. Judgment would come because the people of Judah were spiraling downward in unfaithfulness. They had devolved into syncretistic practices, worshiping Baal on the high places and even offering child sacrifices to Molech. This was abhorrent to the Lord, and he was preparing to pour out his wrath upon them. By this time, Assyria had ruled Judah for more than a century, but Assyria was becoming weaker; Babylon would soon conquer them. Habakkuk prophesied in this tense political climate. He likely lived to witness the destruction of Nineveh by Babylon in 612 BC as well as the battle of Haran (609 BC) and the defeat of the Assyrians at Carchemish (605). He may even have lived to witness the fall of Judah to Babylon in 587.

Zephaniah prophesied during the reforms of King Josiah (640–609 BC), who is described as a king who "did what was right in the eyes of the LORD and walked in all the way of David his father, and he did not turn aside to the right or to the left" (2 Kings 22:2). Through his reforms, Josiah sought to restore the nation of Judah by returning her to covenant fidelity after the reign of the wicked King Manasseh. Ever since the time of Zephaniah's great-grandfather Hezekiah, many in Judah were not worshiping according to God's commands (2 Kings 21:1–26). Josiah restored the temple and reinstituted the Feast of Passover. The nation experienced a brief return to faithful practice, but it did not last. They quickly fell away from the Lord once again after Josiah died. "Israel" is mentioned in Zephaniah 2:9 and 3:13–15, but the northern kingdom had already been taken into exile by Assyria in 722 BC. In these verses, "Israel" refers to Judah and its capital, Jerusalem, which had not yet fallen. Jeremiah, Nahum, and Habakkuk prophesied at the same time, and together they describe the need for spiritual transformation. While the word of the Lord had been declared at many times and in many ways, there were many who still refused to respond in faith and repentance[God's Word is constantly addressing the hardness of the sinful heart with the hope of the gospel of Jesus Christ.]

Outline

Lamentations

I. How Lonely Sits the City (1:1–22)
II. God Has Set Zion under a Cloud (2:1–22)
III. I Am the Man Who Has Seen Affliction (3:1–66)
IV. How the Gold Has Grown Dim (4:1–22)
V. Restore Us to Yourself, O Lord (5:1–22)

Habakkuk

I. Superscription (1:1)
II. First Cycle (1:2–11)
III. Second Cycle (1:12–2:20)
IV. Habakkuk's Prayer (3:1–19)

Zephaniah

I. Heading (1:1)
II. Judgment Coming against Judah (1:2–6)
III. The Day of the Lord (1:7–3:20)

As You Get Started

What is your current understanding of how Lamentations, Habakkuk, and Zephaniah help us comprehend the whole storyline of the Bible? Do you have an idea of how aspects of the books' message are found elsewhere in the Old Testament or fulfilled in the New Testament?

Every book in Scripture, OT & NT, points to Jesus Christ. How He will bring fulfillment & completion, restoration & healing. These books point to the need for a Savior, for Christ's coming, & how God is working even in the days leading up to Jesus.

What is your current understanding of what Lamentations, Habakkuk, and Zephaniah contribute to Christian theology? What might these books teach us about God, Jesus Christ, sin, judgment, redemption, repentance, salvation, or other such doctrines?

They give us a deeper understanding of man's wickedness & God's judgment.
-acknowledge the need for salvation & redemption

What aspects of Lamentations, Habakkuk, or Zephaniah have confused you? Are there any specific questions that you hope this study will help you to answer?

Haven't studied in depth.

As You Finish This Unit . . .

Take a few minutes to ask God to help you understand and apply the truth of Scripture to your life as you begin this study of Lamentations, Habakkuk, and Zephaniah.

Week 2: Pour Out Your Heart to the Lord

Lamentations 1–2

The Place of the Passage

God called Abram and promised to make him the father of many nations (Gen. 12:1–3). God also promised to give him a place in which to dwell (Gen. 12:7). Later, God raised up Moses to lead these people out of Egypt and into the Promised Land (Ex. 3:1–12), establishing a covenant[1] with blessings for obedience and curses for disobedience (Deuteronomy 28–30). God established his people and eventually set them in Zion. But throughout the generations, the people strayed from the Lord. Those unfaithful to the covenant must be purged from the people. God sent the nation of Babylon to judge Judah for her sins, and at the opening of Lamentations, Jerusalem lies in ruins. The nation cries out for help. A narrator speaks in 1:1–9a, 10–11a, and 17 while Jerusalem herself speaks in verses 9b, 11b–16, and 18–22. God's judgment is total, and the people suffer and express great sorrow.

The Big Picture

Judah has been exiled, and the nation mourns the loss of her former glory and cries to the Lord for relief.

> ## Reflection and Discussion

Read through the complete passage for this study, Lamentations 1–2. Then review the questions below concerning this section of Lamentations and write your notes on them. (For further background, see the *ESV Study Bible*, pages 1589–1594; available online at www.esv.org.)

1. Jerusalem's Devastation (1:1–11)

What imagery does the narrator use to describe the pain and sorrow of the nation (vv. 1–11)? What does this indicate about the gravity of their transgression and the severity of their subsequent punishment? *> great*

-like royalty turned to slaves
-friends now enemies
-no rest; constant distress & affliction
-filthy, unclean

What reason is given for Judah's exile (vv. 8–9)?

sin!

2. Jerusalem's Call for Help (1:12–22)

To whom does Jerusalem express her sorrow (vv. 12, 19), and what is her complaint? Does comfort come from those to whom she cries out?

passersby, lovers/friends.
they deceive, lack compassion.

In 1:20–22, the author continues to acknowledge the nation's guilt, but what seems to make the suffering even worse?

enemies are rejoicing in their suffering

3. God Has Set Zion under a Cloud (2:1–22)

What are the effects of God's punishment on Jerusalem (2:1–10)?

destroyed their city, palaces, & houses
taken away everything they found
pleasure & joy in

The narrator cries out for justice to come upon their enemies but then makes a transition in 2:18–19, culminating with a cry to the Lord in 2:20–22. What does this indicate about his source of confidence and hope for the future?

He knows God's power & this character

Lamentations is written by a person with firsthand experience of divine judgment at the "day of the LORD" (see Joel 2:1–2; Amos 5:18; Zeph. 1:14–16). At the same time, he knows the character of God. How is this perspective beneficial for the rest of God's people as they read Scripture?

understanding judgment in light of
God's character is important,

especially as we teach others about it.

Read through the following three sections on *Gospel Glimpses, Whole-Bible Connections*, and *Theological Soundings*. Then take time to consider the *Personal Implications* these sections may have for you.

Gospel Glimpses

HOPE IN DARKNESS. The Bible speaks to our pain through Judah's experience. Imagine being abandoned by all of one's friends, left all alone. Imagine living in a country in which such a situation is not the exception but the rule, with everyone feeling this way. This would be overwhelming, and it would be easy to fall into despair. However sorrowful Lamentations is, it holds up an understanding God. He is not removed from his people but is involved in their lives. He is tenderhearted and cares for them. God's love for us is shown most clearly in how he "did not spare his own Son but gave him up for us all" (Rom. 8:32). Jesus entered into the lives of his people. He is a man of sorrows (Isa. 53:1–12) and the bearer of our sin. Jesus suffers the full exile. As the church, Christ's body, our sufferings in the present life conform us to his sufferings so that we too might share in his subsequent glories (Phil. 3:10). We can have hope amid darkness because he understands our suffering (Heb. 4:15) and has triumphed over the darkness.

Whole-Bible Connections

THE ENEMY. Lamentations begins with the mention of enemies (1:2, 10, 16, 21; 2:3, 7, 16, 17, 22), pursuers (1:3, 6), and foes (1:5, 7, 17). The immediate historical context of these references is Babylon, which laid siege against Jerusalem in 587 BC under Nebuchadnezzar II. But Babylon stands for something much greater and more sinister than the geopolitical forces of that time. This is apparent as we see how the name of Babylon is invoked in the New Testament. Peter speaks of Babylon in 1 Peter 5:13 as the context in which the church lives in exile; he was not writing immediately to people in the geographic region of Babylon. Similarly, John references Babylon several times in the book of Revelation to describe the great enemy of God and his people (Rev. 14:8; 16:19; 17:5; 18:2, 10, 21). John does not expect the nation of Babylon that took the southern kingdom into exile to resurface; rather, Babylon is used as a code name for the kingdom of this world. Babylon embodies this kingdom at the time of Lamentations, but even when this specific empire passes away, others take its place (see Dan. 7:1–8). Rome, for example, is the specific historical referent at the time of the book of Revelation. Nonetheless, God is accomplishing a greater victory through his Son, Jesus Christ. He does not triumph over merely a geopolitical nation but rather over the forces of evil and the "prince of the power of the air" (Eph. 2:2). Through the resurrection, he conquers the last enemy, which is death itself (1 Cor. 15:54–57).

SET APART. God calls his people out from the world. They are not chosen because of anything within themselves. Quite to the contrary, they are unwanted and unloved (Ezek. 16:4–5). But the Lord sets his gracious love upon them (Ezek. 16:6–14). It is for this reason that God's judgment of Judah as described in Lamentations 1–2 is especially harsh—as God's chosen people, called to holiness, the people's rejection of God and their descent into wickedness is particularly blatant. After all, the Scripture makes clear that the Lord chooses Israel from among the nations in order to demonstrate his power and attributes throughout the world. He establishes a covenant with them and calls them to be "a kingdom of priests and a holy nation" (Ex. 19:5–6). In other words, they are to reflect the character of their covenant God. This notion of holiness and distinction is embedded within the ceremonial law. As people come closer to the presence of the Lord, they are called to greater ceremonial purity. The Most Holy Place is most closely identified with God's presence, as there is a special holiness to the innermost part of the temple. Proceeding outward from the Most Holy Place, we find lesser and lesser degrees of holiness. We go to the inner court, then the outer court—then even out into the city of Jerusalem. Finally, outside the city ("outside the camp"; see Heb. 13:11–15) is the worst place to be, because it is the farthest from the Lord's holy presence. These ceremonial degrees of holiness apply also to the people of Israel. The priests are considered the most holy, then the ceremonially clean Jews, particularly men. Then follows the ceremonially clean women, Gentiles, and those who are ceremonially unclean. These general principles of holiness guide the life of Israel and illustrate the difference between God and man and between God's people and the world. God's people are to be pure and are to fellowship closely with him. In the New Testament, the church is called a kingdom of priests and a holy nation (1 Pet. 2:9). They are "sanctified in Christ Jesus" (1 Cor. 1:2), called to reflect the holiness of their Lord.

EXILE. As described in these first two chapters of Lamentations, the nation of Judah acts wickedly. They become unholy and need to be removed from God's holy presence, identified as the Promised Land. Israel was set apart but is now among the nations. They were set in the Promised Land, but now they find no resting place. They seemingly have returned to a darker time in their history, when they were captive in Egypt, subjected to forced labor and restrained from worshiping the Lord as he desired (Ex. 1:1–14; 2:23; 5:11; 6:6, 9). The Lord raised up Moses to lead his people out of slavery and into the Promised Land. This pattern was present in the beginning, when Adam and Eve were exiled from the holy realm of the garden of Eden because of their disobedience. As he bore our sin, Jesus Christ was also "exiled" to death while he led us out of our slavery to sin (Isa. 61:1; Ps. 68:18). He suffered outside the gates of the city, and, in conformity to Christ's sufferings, we participate in this "exile" and are thereby sanctified (Heb. 13:11–15). Christ has restored his people and established them as "a kingdom of priests and a holy nation" (Ex. 19:5–6; compare 1 Pet. 2:9–10).

Theological Soundings

ELECTION. The nation of Judah reveals the biblical doctrine of unconditional election. The people of Judah were not chosen because of any inherent worth or merit. Nor were there any conditions attached to their election. God chose them unconditionally from among the nations and made them the blessed recipients of his covenant love. Likewise, those who receive eternal life through Jesus Christ do not and cannot make themselves suitable for their election. Such election "depends not on human will or exertion, but on God, who has mercy" (Rom. 9:16).

GOD'S JUSTICE. As the Westminster Shorter Catechism puts it, sin is any lack of conformity to or transgression of God's law. Since God is perfectly holy and just, sin must be punished. God was committed to his people, and he gave his commandment and the terms of his covenant to them, but they transgressed those commands and "sinned grievously" (Lam. 1:8). God will not fail to bring about the just punishment for such transgression.

GOD'S BEAUTY. The sin of God's people presents God's beauty in sharp relief. The people are hopeless and devastated, yet the Lord is in control. We know this by the content of the Lord's revelation as well as its literary form. The poetic beauty and order of Lamentations itself encourages us to find hope in the Lord. He protects us from total despair, because beauty and order will triumph over ugliness and chaos.

GOD'S MERCY. Although the nation is being punished for her iniquities, God is merciful. He never ceases to be just, and yet he provides mercy through the Messiah. Jesus Christ bears the penalty for the sins of his people. They are not fugitives from justice. Rather, Christ has borne their iniquities and granted them his righteousness.

Personal Implications

Take time to reflect on the implications of Lamentations 1–2 for your own life today. Write down your reflections under the three headings we have considered and on the passage as a whole.

1. Gospel Glimpses

need for a Savior

2. Whole-Bible Connections

Covenant

Day of the Lord

3. Theological Soundings

4. Lamentations 1–2

As You Finish This Unit . . .

Take a moment now to ask for the Lord's blessing and help as you continue in this study of Lamentations, Habakkuk, and Zephaniah. Take a moment also to look back through this unit of study, to reflect on some key things that the Lord may be teaching you—and perhaps to highlight and underline these things to review again in the future.

Definition

[1] **Covenant** – A binding agreement between two parties, typically involving a formal statement of their relationship, a list of stipulations and obligations for both parties, a list of witnesses to the agreement, and a list of curses for unfaithfulness and blessings for faithfulness to the agreement.

Week 3: God's Inexhaustible Love

Lamentations 3

▲

The Place of the Passage

A single voice speaks in Lamentations 3. This speaker has endured great personal suffering but has also experienced God's enduring faithfulness. He has come to know God's unfailing and unchanging character. In response, he prays for renewal and looks to the future with a confident hope that the Lord will hear his cries and respond.

The Big Picture

The Lord's love for his people can never be exhausted, for he is faithful.

Reflection and Discussion

Read through the complete passage for this study, Lamentations 3. Then review the questions concerning this section of Lamentations and write your notes on them. (For further background, see the *ESV Study Bible*, pages 1595–1598; available online at www.esv.org.)

1. Enduring Suffering and Experiencing Faithfulness (3:1–24)

The speaker feels a great sense of loss (vv. 1–18). What phrases and images does the speaker use to describe his suffering?

People hope in many different things, but the things of this world never fully satisfy. What is the true source of the believer's hope (v. 18; compare Pss. 16:5; 73:26)?

To what does the speaker cling amid this suffering and loss (vv. 19–24)?

2. Responding to God's Goodness and Sovereignty (3:25–39)

Scripture often makes a distinction between God's covenant people and the world. To whom is the Lord good (v. 25)? What does it mean to wait for and seek the Lord (see also Pss. 34:10; 37:1–11; Amos 5:4, 14)?

3. Praying for Renewal (3:40–47)

After acknowledging that the Lord's punishment for sin is just, the speaker exhorts the nation to cry out for God's mercy and forgiveness. What specifically does he tell the people to do (vv. 40–41)?

4. Maintaining Confidence in God (3:48–66)

How does the Lord respond when the speaker cries out to him (vv. 55–57)? How does the Lord take up his cause (vv. 58–66)?

Read through the following three sections on *Gospel Glimpses, Whole-Bible Connections*, and *Theological Soundings*. Then take time to consider the *Personal Implications* these sections may have for you.

Gospel Glimpses

FATHERLY DISCIPLINE. Although Babylon brought this destruction upon Judah, these enemies were instruments in God's hand. This truth was difficult for the people of Judah to understand, especially since they were the chosen people of God. The Lord chastised his people for repeated and willful sin. Indeed, "It is good for a man that he bear the yoke in his youth" (Lam. 3:27). However, God's discipline does not compromise his goodness toward his people. Rather, God's grace is evident in this passage. Even as he disciplines, he is compassionate, for his fatherly discipline flows out of his love (Heb. 12:5ff.). He is doing what is best for his people. Therefore, when we are disciplined similarly, we should not

23

argue with God (Lam. 3:39). God is just, and when he punishes sin, we have no reason to complain.

GOD'S ENDURING LOVE. The author declares, "The steadfast love of the LORD never ceases" (Lam. 3:22). This is rich covenantal language found throughout the Old Testament. The Hebrew word translated "steadfast love" is *hesed*, which conveys a deep sense of the Lord's abiding faithfulness to his people. This is tremendously encouraging, for while humans often waver, God is not fickle. His love is not at the mercy of changing moods. It is steadfast, "for the LORD is good; his steadfast love endures forever, and his faithfulness to all generations" (Ps. 100:5). Though the Lord is just, he is also merciful. He forgives the sins of his people, and his judgment is replaced by restoration.

DAILY MERCIES. The Lord provides for those in need. His mercies are new every morning (Lam. 3:23). After the exodus from Egypt, Israel wandered in the wilderness. The Lord provided manna for them each day. In the New Testament, Jesus taught his disciples to pray for a similar provision of daily bread (Matt. 6:11). This includes basic sustenance in terms of food and shelter, but God's provision also comes in the form of daily mercies. God's daily mercies remind us of his faithfulness. Rather than giving us a lifetime of mercies in an instant that we could store away, the Lord establishes a relationship with us. He desires us to come to him daily so that we learn of his love for us and of our need of him each moment. And as we come to him, we can also be confident that we will never exhaust his mercies. They are *new every* morning. There is new mercy for his people every day.

Whole-Bible Connections

JESUS THE SUFFERER. The "darkness" in Lamentations 3:6 foreshadows the "day of the Lord" (compare Joel 2:1–2; Amos 5:18; Zeph. 1:14–16). This is a key phrase used throughout the Prophets to refer to a great day of judgment in which the Lord would pour out his wrath upon all sin. The Prophets speak of multiple instances of the "day of the Lord," indicating that the Lord's judgment comes several times in anticipation of a final day of judgment. For example, God came in judgment upon Judah in 587 BC, but that did not resolve the problem of sin once and for all. God's wrath is still stored up for the ultimate day of the Lord, which will mark the end of this present evil age. It will be the final judgment, a separation of the sheep and the goats, the wheat and the tares (Matt. 13:24–30; 25:31–46; Rev. 21:7–8). Jesus brings this justice upon his enemies (Rev. 19:11–16), but the one who has faith in Jesus Christ escapes final judgment precisely because Christ paid the penalty for sin (Gal. 2:20; Rom. 5:1–6).

AN EVERLASTING INHERITANCE. Lamentations expresses the anguish of God's people, who have been exiled from the land. This was catastrophic to the ancient people, since their livelihood, heritage, and inheritance were identified with that locale. But Lamentations compels God's people to look deeper, to the greater significance of the land in the purposes of God. When the Lord spoke to Aaron in Numbers 18:20, he said that his sons would not receive a land inheritance but that the Lord would be the portion for the tribe of Levi. This demonstrated a reality that is true for all of God's people. By the time of Lamentations, Judah had been exiled, yet the faithful had not lost their true inheritance because it still is found in the Lord. The land itself was not the greatest blessing; it served as the venue for the blessed presence of the Lord. This point is made in chapters 3–4 and 11–12 of Hebrews, which speak of the believer's heavenly rest. God's desire is to bring his people into his holy presence, but it is not possible for them to enter that rest in their sinful condition (Heb. 12:14). Only those who trust in Christ will be saved and brought into this heavenly rest through his mediation.

Theological Soundings

GOD'S CHARACTER. Theologians speak of God's immutability, or his unchangeableness. He is the same yesterday, today, and forever (see Heb. 13:8). His being is utterly distinct from that of his creatures, who are entirely dependent on him and who change from moment to moment. Since God is unchanging, he is reliable and consistent in everything he says and does. Indeed, he cannot lie (Titus 1:2). This is the foundation upon which we can be confident in God's promises. His steadfast love (covenant mercy) never ceases. This is the reason the author of Lamentations can say that the steadfast love of the Lord remains with the people (3:22). God's love for his people is not dependent on their performance. It depends on God alone. How then can God love the ungodly? It is possible only through Jesus Christ, who suffered and died on behalf of his people (Isa. 53:1–6) and thereby gave them a righteousness by which the ungodly may be justified (Rom. 4:5). This is God's unfailing character: to love his people despite themselves. "In this is love, not that we have loved God but that he loved us and sent his Son to be the propitiation for our sins" (1 John 4:10).

THE FORGIVENESS OF SINS. The people of Judah may have preferred that God would overlook their sins while pouring out his wrath on their enemies. But God cannot forget the sins of his people by pretending a transgression never occurred. This seems to present a problem, because if the people must endure the full wrath of God for their sins, then the steadfast love of the Lord would cease. There would be a morning in which it was not there. However, God can remain true to his covenant promises because he addresses the sins of his people through Jesus Christ. Jesus paid the debt of his people in full by his obedience and death. His blood covers their sins so that they are forgiven. He has redeemed their lives (Lam. 3:58). While they may fall under God's fatherly displeasure for a time, they will never fall from the state of justification. God will restore them as they confess their sins in faith and repentance.

> ## Personal Implications

Take time to reflect on the implications of Lamentations 3 for your own life today. Write down your reflections under the three headings we have considered and on the passage as a whole.

1. Gospel Glimpses

2. Whole-Bible Connections

3. Theological Soundings

4. Lamentations 3

As You Finish This Unit . . .

Take a moment now to ask for the Lord's blessing and help as you continue in this study of Lamentations, Habakkuk, and Zephaniah. Take a moment also to look back through this unit of study, to reflect on some key things that the Lord may be teaching you—and perhaps to highlight and underline these things to review again in the future.

WEEK 4: EXILED NO LONGER

Lamentations 4

The Place of the Passage

The fourth chapter of Lamentations describes the experience of several different groups among the nation of Judah as they experience exile. The suffering is so bad that even children suffer at the hands of their parents. Rulers and the wealthy have fallen far from their positions of power and glory, and their overconfidence has withered to despair. The enemies have demonstrated their power and superiority, and some continue to gloat over Judah's plight. Amid it all, the Lord promises rest and relief. He will bring an end to his people's exile while visiting judgment upon the wicked.

The Big Picture

God promises an end to suffering and injustice.

> **Reflection and Discussion**

Read through the complete passage for this study, Lamentations 4. Then review the questions below concerning this section of Lamentations and write your notes on them. (For further background, see the *ESV Study Bible*, pages 1598–1600; available online at www.esv.org.)

1. The Children Suffer (4:1–10)

The speaker contrasts the present suffering of Jerusalem's children with their former status (vv. 1–5, 7–8). Describe their former condition in relation to their current suffering.

We know that the people suffer because of their sins, but the prophet describes the degree of their sinfulness using new imagery in chapter 4. How wicked has Judah become? How does the prophet describe their actions in relation to animals (v. 3)?

Sodom is notorious in the Old Testament for its wickedness, yet the people of Judah have acted even more wickedly. Why and how was the punishment of Jerusalem greater than that of Sodom (v. 6)?

2. The Leaders Are Punished (4:11–16)

What were the sins of Israel's prophets and priests? What was the result of their shedding the blood of the righteous (vv. 14–16)?

3. Powerful Enemies (4:17–20)

How does the prophet describe the enemies' prowess (vv. 18–19)? Since they are instruments in God's hands to bring judgment upon sin, what does this description say about God's justice on the day of the Lord (see Joel 2:1–2; Amos 5:18; Zeph. 1:14–16)?

4. The End of Suffering (4:21–22)

Jerusalem can rejoice that her punishment is complete, but what will be the fate of nations that have rejoiced over Jerusalem's punishment?

Read through the following three sections on *Gospel Glimpses*, *Whole-Bible Connections*, and *Theological Soundings*. Then take time to consider the *Personal Implications* these sections may have for you.

Gospel Glimpses

THE LORD'S COMMITMENT. Judah is suffering and searching for help in all quarters. She will receive no aid from her allies (v. 17), no escape will succeed (vv. 18–19), and her king will be of no help (v. 20). Judah has placed her hope in these things, but they have all failed. Verse 17 reminds the people to look to the Lord, for they have misplaced their confidence. Although the nation has been driven away from his holy presence, God has not forgotten his people. He had every reason to abandon them, but this is not his character. He has established a covenant with them and is committed to them such that he overcomes their transgressions through his grace.

HOPE FOR THE FUTURE. With all of their favorite options exhausted, the people seem to be hopeless. Nonetheless, there is hope for the future because God reveals his grace. The Lord declares that he will keep them in exile no longer (v. 22). With darkness closing in on all sides, this would have been astounding news, but this is exactly how the Lord works. His grace enters like a ray of light shattering the darkness. His "power is made perfect in weakness" (2 Cor. 12:9). History reveals that God's word was accomplished soon thereafter, when the Jews began to return from exile between 538 and 535 BC.

Whole-Bible Connections

GOD'S GRACIOUS PROMISE. God's redemptive love for his people has been expressed throughout the ages. It was revealed as early as Genesis 3:15, just after Adam and Eve fell into sin. God promised to overcome their sin by the "offspring" of the woman, who would crush the head of the serpent. In that gracious promise, God established a firm commitment to his people from which he would not depart. This promise was established further with Abraham, who would become the father of many nations. God brought Abraham's progeny into the Land of Promise and commanded them to walk in his ways (Deut. 30:1–10). Centuries later, Judah departed from the Lord, and they are judged accordingly (Lam. 4:6, 11, 16). But their sin—as great as it was—could not void God's promises. Those who believe in the coming Messiah are still identified with Abraham. He is the father of all who believe (Gen. 15:1–6; 17:1–8; Rom. 4:11–12; Gal. 3:29). Judah would forfeit her provisional dwelling in the Promised Land, but that does not mean she would forfeit the promise of eternal life. Abraham himself looked to a "city that has foundations" (see Heb. 11:8–10), which would be revealed as the heavenly Mount Zion (Heb. 12:18–24). And as God's people continue to trust in him, they too have an eternal resting place.

SONS OF GOD. Adam (Luke 3:38) and Israel (Ex. 4:22) were "sons of God," but they failed to obey the Lord perfectly. Adam was placed in the garden of Eden with the command not to eat of the tree of the knowledge of good and evil (Gen. 2:16–17). He transgressed God's law and was exiled from the holy realm (Gen. 3:22–24). Later, God established a covenant with the people of Israel, who were given the Promised Land as a blessing with the provision that they would obey the Lord according to his covenant (Deuteronomy 28–30). Like Adam before them, they disobeyed and were exiled. The die had been cast, and it became painfully obvious that God's people were lost on account of their sinfulness. But God did not forsake his people (see Lam. 4:22). He sent his eternal Son, Jesus Christ, who succeeded at every point in which Adam and Israel had failed. This is one reason the apostle Paul calls Jesus the "last Adam" (1 Cor. 15:45). While the first Adam became identified with sin, the last Adam is identified with righteousness, peace, and redemption. Christ saves his people from the sins committed under the first covenant and establishes a new covenant in his blood (see 1 Cor. 11:25; Heb. 9:11–15). He is the true Israel (Isa. 11:1–2; Matt. 2:13–15), and believers become sons of God through him (Rom. 8:14–15, 19, 29).

> ## Theological Soundings

REPENTANCE AND RESTORATION. It is evident throughout Lamentations that God punishes sin. Since God is holy, sin stands as a barrier between us and him. As sinners, there is no way for us to approach God on our own account. But that sin need not be the end of the story. We are not without hope because God is compassionate, and those who fall into sin may ask the Lord for forgiveness. As they turn away from their sin and turn to God, they seek restoration. Forgiveness always involves restoration, since forgiveness is the righting of an offense one person has committed against another (Matt. 18:21–22; Eph. 4:32). By forgiving the offense, the barrier has been removed and restoration becomes possible. God promised to restore the repentant nation, and Jerusalem may take comfort that her punishment has come to an end (Lam. 4:22).

THE SHAME OF SIN. The good news for Judah is that the daughter of Zion will be exiled no longer. This is described in contrast to Edom, whose sins will be uncovered (v. 22). Nebuchadnezzar of Babylon had given Edom the rural areas of Judah after the exile as a reward for not siding with Judah. And so, while Judah was being judged, Edom took great delight. They gloated over Judah in her downfall. But Edom's joy would be short-lived, because they would also receive God's justice. This is described as nakedness and shame, imagery found throughout the Scriptures. After the fall into sin, Adam and Eve's eyes were opened, and they knew that they were naked (Gen. 3:7). While they were physically naked, there was also something much deeper in view, for Adam and Eve were not previously unaware of their lack of physical clothing. After their fall into sin, they had become naked in a new way: they had lost their innocence, their original glory. Shame had come upon them for having sinned against God. The apostle Paul also invokes this imagery when he indicates his desire not to be ashamed on the last day (Phil. 1:20). He is not speaking in mere psychological or sentimental terms. He is instead speaking of his standing before the Lord. At the final judgment, all sins will be exposed, which will result in public shame. On that day, sinners will be naked before the Lord, but in Christ we have a covering for sin. Just as the Lord provided animal skins for Adam and Eve (Gen. 3:21), believers are clothed in Christ's righteousness (Eph. 4:20–24; Phil. 3:9).

Personal Implications

Take time to reflect on the implications of Lamentations 4 for your own life today. Write down your reflections under the three headings we have considered and on the passage as a whole.

1. Gospel Glimpses

2. Whole-Bible Connections

3. Theological Soundings

4. Lamentations 4

As You Finish This Unit . . .

Take a moment now to ask for the Lord's blessing and help as you continue in this study of Lamentations, Habakkuk, and Zephaniah. Take a moment also to look back through this unit of study, to reflect on some key things that the Lord may be teaching you—and perhaps to highlight and underline these things to review again in the future.

WEEK 5: THE FUTURE RESTORATION

Lamentations 5

The Place of the Passage

This is the final poem of the book of Lamentations. The prophet lifts up his voice in prayer to the Lord, asking him to hear and respond to the cries of his people.

The Big Picture

Though Judah's suffering is overwhelming, there is hope because God restores his people.

Reflection and Discussion

Read through the complete passage for this study, Lamentations 5. Then review the questions concerning this section of Lamentations and write your notes on them. (For further background, see the *ESV Study Bible*, pages 1600–1602; available online at www.esv.org.)

1. Jerusalem's Woes (5:1–18)

The people remind the Lord of the economic, social, and political suffering and disgrace they have faced. What has happened to their inheritance?

List the humiliations shown to various groups of people in the nation of Judah (vv. 11–14).

What is the significance of the city gate in this culture? What has happened to it (v. 14)?

The people of Judah lack basic provisions such as food, water, and shelter (vv. 4, 9–10). They have no rest or peace (vv. 5, 13) and enjoy no freedom (vv. 7–8). How does the author describe the attitude of the people because of this lack (vv. 15, 17)?

In what ways does Mount Zion lie desolate (1:4, 16; 3:11; 4:5)?

2. Prayer for Restoration (5:19–22)

Who is the nation's only hope for restoration and forgiveness (vv. 19, 21)?

How does the activity of prayer relate to restoration with God (v. 21)?

In light of God's promises in Leviticus 26:44–45, Deuteronomy 30:1–10, Isaiah 57:14–21, Jeremiah 31–32, and Hosea 11:1–9, is it possible for God to reject utterly and remain exceedingly angry with Judah (Lam. 5:22)?

Read through the following three sections on *Gospel Glimpses, Whole-Bible Connections*, and *Theological Soundings*. Then take time to consider the *Personal Implications* these sections may have for you.

Gospel Glimpses

GOD'S SOVEREIGNTY. Whatever has happened to Israel and Judah has not altered the Lord's cosmic rule. His throne endures to all generations (Lam. 5:19; compare Ps. 123:1–2). The people of other nations at the time of Lamentations believed their gods' fate was bound up with earthly events. Many of Judah's neighbors were "henotheists." That is, they believed in the existence of many gods though they often worshiped only one. Moreover, many believed that each god was sovereign over a geographic region. Therefore, if one nation defeated another, it was an indication that the victorious nation's god had defeated the other nation's god. The Scriptures reject this notion. Moses delivered the word of the Lord to the people, saying, "Hear, O Israel: The LORD our God, the LORD is one. You shall love the LORD your God with all your heart and with all your soul and with all your might" (Deut. 6:4–5). This is indeed an affirmation that God is one god and not many. But it is also a statement that God is the *only* god. No others exist. Even though Babylon has taken Judah into exile, Yahweh still reigns (Lam. 5:19). Indeed, he is the one who sent Babylon as an instrument to chastise his people. No matter our earthly circumstances, we can be confident that the Lord is sovereign and in control. God—the only god—has his purposes: "We know that for those who love God all things work together for good, for those who are called according to his purpose" (Rom. 8:28).

THE LORD'S ANGER. The prophet cries out, "Why do you forget us forever, why do you forsake us for so many days?" (Lam. 5:20). This verse is instructive for our prayers. We must not be afraid to pour out our hearts to the Lord, for the Lord does not remain angry forever (Ps. 30:5). We can ask the Lord questions such as this, but we cannot demand answers. We can bring our complaints to God, but we must not complain about him. The prophet communicates his true feelings to the Lord, asking that he would bring this time of harsh discipline to an end. God shows his grace to his people by hearing their cries and restoring them.

Whole-Bible Connections

A GREATER RESTORATION. Mount Zion was the location of the temple and the ark of the covenant, where God was specially present in the Promised Land. Although at this point in Lamentations Zion lies desolate, and jackals prowl over it (5:18), God has not forgotten his promises. While the book of Lamentations is the cry of God's people amid terrible suffering, it ends with in the confidence that the Lord will reign forever. From that foundation, the author pleads for restoration. And we know from history that the Lord hears his prayers and responds. The Jews begin to return from exile between 538 and 535 BC, and they rebuild the city and construct a second temple. Nonetheless, when it is completed, "Many of the priests and Levites and heads of fathers' houses, old men who had seen the first house, wept with a loud voice when they saw the foundation of this house being laid" (Ezra 3:12). This new temple could not compare to the glory of the temple that had been destroyed. This would have been utterly disappointing because it would have seemed to be only a partial restoration, paling in comparison to the previous condition of Jerusalem. But this would be an important lesson to the people, because there is yet a greater fulfillment and a consummate restoration that will come with the new heavens and the new earth (Isa. 65:17ff.). The greatest blessing from the Lord is neither to dwell in the land per se nor to enjoy the presence of the Lord mediated through Old Testament types and shadows; it is, rather, to be in the glorious presence of God for eternity (Ps. 84:10; Rev. 22:1–5).

SUFFERING UNTO GLORY. Lamentations is a book filled with sorrow. Yet, as David declares, "Weeping may tarry for the night, but joy comes with the morning" (Ps. 30:5). The Lord triumphs over the suffering of his people. In the Sermon on the Mount, Jesus teaches, "Blessed are those who mourn, for they shall be comforted" (Matt. 5:4). True comfort comes through Jesus Christ. Christ himself demonstrates the pattern of life for God's people, which is a life of humiliation unto exaltation, of suffering unto glory (Phil. 2:5–11). God's people are being conformed to his image (Rom. 8:29), which entails being conformed to his sufferings so that we too might share in his subsequent glories (Phil. 3:10–11; 1 Pet. 1:11).

Theological Soundings

REGENERATION. In Lamentations 5, it is critical to acknowledge that God is the initiator of restoration. God does not react to his people. By his grace, *he acts first* in the lives of his people. This is demonstrated most clearly in the biblical doctrine of regeneration,[1] which is the work of the Spirit to bring a sinner to life. Jesus declares, "Unless one is born again he cannot see the kingdom of God" (John 3:3). The Holy Spirit must first bring to life a person who is dead in his or her sins. Dead people do not approach God first, only to have God react to their prompting. Rather, God initiates salvation by his grace. Having then been regenerated by the Holy Spirit, God's people are convinced of their sin, enlightened in their minds, and renewed in their wills. They are brought to repent and believe on Jesus Christ for their salvation. But God is not merely the initiator of salvation, leaving his people to do the rest. All of salvation is a gift of God (Eph. 2:8). This provides great comfort to those who have faith in Christ, because salvation does not depend on the one being saved. The Lord begins the good work in his people and will bring it to completion at the day of Jesus Christ (Phil. 1:6).

DOCTRINE AND LIFE. When we consider theological topics such as regeneration, we may be tempted to focus solely on the intellectual aspects of such a study. But restoration unto the Lord involves more than an intellectual change. It involves a whole-life transformation. This is demonstrated in the way the biblical authors speak of knowledge. Knowledge is not mere information we may attain; it is also a condition of the heart. For example, to "know" God is not merely to know about him, but to believe, love, and obey him. God is not concerned with mere intellectual knowledge any more than he is with mere outward conformity to the law (James 2:19; Ps. 51:17). His work of grace transforms the entire person, giving them a new heart from which good works will flow (Ezek. 36:26; James 2:14–18; Gal. 5:6). The Lord is concerned with orthodoxy (right doctrine) as well as orthopraxy (right practice). This involves public and private worship as well as faithfulness to God's Word in all aspects of life.

Personal Implications

Take time to reflect on the implications of Lamentations 5 for your own life today. Write down your reflections under the three headings we have considered and on the passage as a whole.

1. Gospel Glimpses

2. Whole-Bible Connections

3. Theological Soundings

_____

_____

_____

_____

_____

4. Lamentations 5

_____

_____

_____

_____

_____

As You Finish This Unit . . .

Take a moment now to ask for the Lord's blessing and help as you continue in this study of Lamentations, Habakkuk, and Zephaniah. Take a moment also to look back through this unit of study, to reflect on some key things that the Lord may be teaching you—and perhaps to highlight and underline these things to review again in the future.

Definition

[1] **Regeneration** – The Holy Spirit's work of bringing spiritual life to a person, thus enabling him or her to love and follow God. Essentially equivalent to what is often referred to as being "born again" or "saved."

Week 6: God's Answer to Prayer

Habakkuk 1:1–11

The Place of the Passage

Habakkuk cries out to the Lord for help (1:2–4), but the Lord responds that he has already begun answering Habakkuk's prayer (vv. 5–11). Indeed, he responds to Habakkuk, "I am doing a work in your days that you would not believe if told" (v. 5). God is raising up foreign powers as instruments in his hand to bring justice and peace[1] to his people.

The Big Picture

The Lord knows our need before we do, and he is working to bless his people.

Reflection and Discussion

Read through the complete passage for this study, Habakkuk 1:1–11. Then review the questions below concerning this section of Habakkuk and write your notes on them. (For further background, see the *ESV Study Bible*, pages 1849–1850; available online at www.esv.org.)

1. Habakkuk's First Lament (1:2–4)

Why does Habakkuk cry out to the Lord? What is his complaint?

Habakkuk uses God's covenant name, "the LORD." What significance does this have, and why would the prophet address the Lord as such?

2. God's Response (1:5–11)

What does it mean for the Chaldeans' (another name for the Babylonians) "justice and dignity [to] go forth from themselves" (v. 7)?

What imagery does the Lord use to describe the power of the coming forces? How does this compare to the Lord's own power?

In what did the Babylonians trust (v. 11)? They have been raised up by the Lord to judge his people, but he will still deal with them for their own transgressions. How does the Babylonians' trust foreshadow their future (v. 10; compare Psalm 2)? Does their future look similar to that of the wicked rulers of Judah itself?

Read through the following three sections on *Gospel Glimpses*, *Whole-Bible Connections*, and *Theological Soundings*. Then take time to consider the *Personal Implications* these sections may have for you.

▶ Gospel Glimpses

ANSWERED PRAYER. God's people had fallen into grave sin. As a nation, they had abandoned the Lord, and he would now bring the covenant curses upon his people. Yet he is gracious and has heard the cries of his servant Habakkuk and others who have looked to him in faith. He was at work to bless his people even before they had cried out to him. In Romans 8, the apostle Paul teaches that the Holy Spirit "helps us in our weakness. For we do not know what to pray for as we ought, but the Spirit himself intercedes for us with groanings too deep for words" (Rom. 8:26). This is a wonderful truth: God has our best interest in mind

(Rom. 8:28). He sent the Holy Spirit to help his people in many ways, not the least of which is in prayer. Paul continues, "And he who searches hearts knows what is the mind of the Spirit, because the Spirit intercedes for the saints according to the will of God" (Rom. 8:27). Even when we fail to understand how to pray or what we need, the Holy Spirit, who knows us more deeply than we know ourselves, intercedes for us according to God's will (1 Cor. 2:10–13).

SURPRISING GRACE. God's grace transcends our understanding. He challenges Habakkuk to "wonder and be astounded," for he is "doing a work . . . that you would not believe if told" (Hab. 1:5). A temptation in prayer can be to tell God how he should answer. This presumes that we know what we need in any given circumstance. However, in Isaiah the Lord declares, "My thoughts are not your thoughts, neither are your ways my ways, declares the LORD. For as the heavens are higher than the earth, so are my ways higher than your ways and my thoughts than your thoughts" (Isa. 55:8–9). We cannot comprehend God's ways. Since he is kind and compassionate toward his people, we cannot comprehend the manifold ways in which he desires to bless us. God surprises his people and exceeds their greatest expectations. Paul cites Habakkuk 1:5 in Acts 13:41 as he preaches the marvelous work of Christ. Grace is receiving that which we do not deserve, and, when received from God, it is also that which we cannot fully comprehend.

Whole-Bible Connections

HABAKKUK'S BURDEN. Verse 1 indicates that Habakkuk is given an "oracle" from God. In other portions of Scripture, this word is used to describe a "burden" (see Ex. 23:5; 2 Kings 5:17; 8:9). Habakkuk is given a great burden from the Lord in the sense that he is obligated to carry this word to the people. He is called to declare the destruction of his own people and their land. This burden becomes even more difficult to carry as Habakkuk wrestles with the truth of God's sovereignty. What if God does things we think are contrary to his character? And so, the prophet dialogues with God. This is natural, and even is encouraged by the Lord, who desires his people to come to him in prayer. The Christian life is a struggle, and it is not easy to walk by faith. The apostle Paul knew this difficulty: "We are afflicted in every way, but not crushed; perplexed, but not driven to despair; persecuted, but not forsaken; struck down, but not destroyed" (2 Cor. 4:8–9). It is only because of Christ that we are not driven to despair. Paul continues that he and Timothy were "always carrying in the body the death of Jesus, so that the life of Jesus may also be manifested in our bodies" (2 Cor. 4:10). "Carrying" the death of Jesus is also a burden, but it is one through which Christ's life will be manifested. Jesus said, "Come to me, all who labor and are heavy laden, and I will give you rest" (Matt. 11:28).

GOOD FROM EVIL. Habakkuk's experience is another example of how the Lord uses the wicked to accomplish good. In Genesis 50:19–20, Joseph spoke with his brothers, who had previously sold him into slavery. Now that he was a powerful and influential leader in Egypt, they feared he might bring retribution upon them and their families. "But Joseph said to them, 'Do not fear, for am I in the place of God? As for you, you meant evil against me, but God meant it for good, to bring it about that many people should be kept alive, as they are today.'" Joseph was a type of Christ. His life foreshadowed and prefigured the sufferings of Christ and his subsequent exaltation to bless his people. While others meant evil against Jesus, God meant it for good. Christ was crucified only to be raised from the dead for the salvation of his people. In the midst of suffering, it appears that the wicked have triumphed. But the Lord uses the wicked as an instrument to accomplish his plans. He moves mysteriously but always succeeds in his time, according to his plan.

Theological Soundings

PRAYER. This passage demonstrates the effectiveness of prayer and the responsiveness of God. Although God is immutable (see "Theological Soundings" on Lamentations 3), he relates to his people. He is the same yesterday, today, and forever (see Heb. 13:8), but he has determined to relate to his people. And so, our prayers to the Lord do not fall upon deaf or unresponsive ears, because he responds according to his will (Hab. 1:5–11). Prayer is the framework by which we express our burdens to God.

DIVINE AND HUMAN KNOWLEDGE. God is omniscient and incomprehensible. Human knowledge is real and true, but it differs from God's knowledge in significant ways. God is the original and ultimate knower, whereas humans are finite and creaturely knowers. Rather than rushing to judge God, we must consider our relation to him as creatures. We must also consider the "big picture" in relation to God's promises. Sometimes it looks like the wicked are "winning," but God has a plan, which he has revealed to his people through creation (Ps. 19:1–2), his Word (2 Tim. 3:16; 2 Pet. 1:16–21), and, ultimately, in his Son, Jesus Christ (Heb. 1:1–4).

Personal Implications

Take time to reflect on the implications of Habakkuk 1:1–11 for your own life today. Write down your reflections under the three headings we have considered and on the passage as a whole.

1. Gospel Glimpses

2. Whole-Bible Connections

3. Theological Soundings

4. Habakkuk 1:1–11

As You Finish This Unit . . .

Take a moment now to ask for the Lord's blessing and help as you continue in this study of Lamentations, Habakkuk, and Zephaniah. Take a moment also to look back through this unit of study, to reflect on some key things that the Lord may be teaching you—and perhaps to highlight and underline these things to review again in the future.

Definition

[1] **Peace** – In modern use, the absence of tension or conflict. In biblical use, a condition of well-being or wholeness that God grants his people, which also results in harmony with God and others.

WEEK 7: THE RIGHTEOUS SHALL LIVE BY HIS FAITH

Habakkuk 1:12–2:20

▲

The Place of the Passage

Having learned of God's plan to use the Babylonians to bring justice to Judah, Habakkuk struggles to understand how God could use a wicked nation to judge a nation that is seemingly less wicked. The Lord's righteousness[1] is vindicated as he punishes the wicked and justifies the one who lives by faith.

The Big Picture

While it appears that evil is going unpunished, in his time the Lord brings justice to all by sparing the ones who live by faith in him.

▶ Reflection and Discussion

Read through the complete passage for this study, Habakkuk 1:12–2:20. Then review the questions below concerning this section of Habakkuk and write your notes on them. (For further background, see the *ESV Study Bible*, pages 1850–1853; available online at www.esv.org.)

1. Habakkuk's Second Lament (1:12–2:1)

What does Habakkuk's second complaint disclose about his knowledge of God's character (vv. 12–13)?

Why is Habakkuk troubled by the Lord's decision to use Babylon to bring judgment on Judah (vv. 15–17)?

Where has Habakkuk stationed himself in 2:1? What is he doing, and what does this indicate about his hope and expectations?

2. God's Response (2:2–20)

What does the Lord's response beginning in verse 2 indicate about his intended audience? To whom is he speaking, ultimately?

What does it mean for the righteous to "live by his faith" (2:4; see also Rom. 1:17; Gal. 3:11; Heb. 10:38)?

In what do the wicked ultimately trust (v. 18)?

Why does Babylon deserve its coming punishment (vv. 6, 9, 12, 15, 19)?

Read through the following three sections on *Gospel Glimpses, Whole-Bible Connections*, and *Theological Soundings*. Then take time to consider the *Personal Implications* these sections may have for you.

Gospel Glimpses

THE LORD'S PLAN. The fulfillment of God's prophecy would not come immediately; it awaited "its appointed time" (Hab. 2:2–3). Therefore, Habakkuk was to be patient (v. 3). Judah would be judged soon, but judgment upon the Babylonians would come later. God is gracious to reveal his plan to Habakkuk. As it did generations ago, God's Word calms our restless hearts and provides comfort today.

DIVINE CHASTISEMENT. God treats his people according to his covenant love. He chastises his people for sin, and the judgment he sends at the hands of the Babylonians is meant to move his people to trust in him rather than in themselves. Even though it is meant for good, however, chastisement is still painful. Habakkuk had asked for the Lord's justice, but the Lord's response seems too strong. To Habakkuk, this appears to be an entire reversal of God's covenant mercies toward his people. A nation seemingly more wicked than Judah will carry Judah away. And yet, divine chastisement must be received in humility; the recipient must acknowledge that the ways of the Lord are good and wise. The Lord is gracious even to correct the sins of his people.

Whole-Bible Connections

GOD'S ETERNAL PLAN. Confidence in the Lord must be rooted in his eternal being. In Habakkuk 1:12–13, the prophet asks a question similar to the statement the Lord makes through the prophet Isaiah when Hezekiah doubts him: "Have you not heard that I determined it long ago? I planned from days of old what now I bring to pass, that you should turn fortified cities into heaps of ruins" (2 Kings 19:25; compare Isa. 37:26). Habakkuk thinks the judgment at hand conflicts with the Lord's eternal election of Israel; it appears to him that the Lord would destroy them utterly, which would make his choice of Israel meaningless. But the Lord has greater plans for Habakkuk and his people. Through the prophet Micah, he declares that a ruler would rise out of Bethlehem who was "from of old" (eternity), "from ancient days" (Mic. 5:2). Daniel speaks also of the "Ancient of Days" (Dan. 7:9). This figure would come from the line of David, but he would not be an ordinary deliverer or a mere earthly leader. He is the Son of God, David's son and David's Lord (Matt. 22:45; Acts 2:34). All of Israel's kings have failed, but Jesus, as King of kings, accomplishes the eternal purposes of the Lord. All the promises of God find their "Yes" in him (2 Cor. 1:20).

LIVING BY FAITH. Habakkuk may be understood to be asking for preferential treatment for the people of God. While they experience a special relationship to the Lord, no one deserves preferential treatment in terms of God's justice, for "all have sinned and fall short of the glory of God" (Rom 3:23). The discriminating factor in how God treats mankind is their relationship to the Savior, Jesus Christ. Those who believe upon him for salvation have a righteousness not their own. More than that, they have a fundamentally different way of life: "The righteous shall live by his faith" (Hab. 2:4). The apostle Paul refers to this passage several times in his epistles (Rom. 1:17; Gal. 3:11; compare Eph. 2:8). Far from being an incidental statement in Habakkuk, this passage declares the profound truth of the believer's new mode of life in Christ. He or she lives by faith (2 Cor. 5:7; Eph. 2:4–10). People speak often of faith in general as referring to believing in something we cannot perceive with the senses. But faith in general is meaningless. Faith is only *saving faith* if it has the proper object. That is, it truly matters only if it is faith *in Christ*. Saving faith is an abiding trust in God that he will accomplish all that he has promised to do. Jesus Christ is the object of saving faith, for he has been faithful to establish a new covenant in his own blood, having died for the sins of his people and having been raised for their salvation. The one who believes on Jesus will be spared from judgment, for he shares the perfect righteousness of Christ (Gal. 2:16; Phil. 3:9).

> ## Theological Soundings

GOD'S BEING AND ATTRIBUTES. Habakkuk struggles to understand how an all-powerful and righteous God could allow sin to continue (1:13). Unknowingly, he ventures toward a biblical answer in his response to the Lord by asking, "Are you not from everlasting, O LORD my God, my Holy One?" (v. 12). Two significant divine attributes are invoked in his question. First, God is eternal (Ps. 90:2). He is not bound by time or the succession of moments. Whereas our lives unfold over the course of time, God perfectly possesses the content of all eternity in a single, indivisible present. Second, God is holy, which refers to his utter perfection and purity. These attributes underscore that God's being is categorically different from ours. He transcends our understanding. Therefore, when Habakkuk considers the present circumstances, he should realize that God's righteousness is not implicated by his actions in history. The present suffering of God's people and the apparent victory of the wicked is not an indictment against God's goodness or power. To the contrary, his righteousness will be vindicated.

IMPUTATION. All humans are sinners. While there are differing degrees of punishment (see, e.g., Matt. 11:21–22), all people deserve God's wrath and curse. But the good news of the gospel is that, because of Christ, we do not have to live on our own merits. We may live by faith in Jesus Christ. This demonstrates the biblical doctrine of imputation (2 Cor. 5:19; Rom. 5:19; 6:11). Imputation is the act of crediting or reckoning. When a sinner believes on Jesus Christ for salvation, God "credits" or "reckons" his or her sin to Jesus while crediting

Jesus' perfect righteousness to the sinner (2 Cor. 5:21). But although saved sinners are viewed as righteous in Christ, they still struggle with sin. As Martin Luther captured so succinctly, they are simultaneously just and sinners. The righteousness imputed to them is outside of themselves. In other words, the righteousness by which we are saved is not based on our own actions. It is a gift of God received by faith and based on the person and work of Jesus Christ.

JUDGMENT. A judgment is an assessment of something or someone, especially as a moral assessment. This occurs in various forms throughout salvation history. The Bible also speaks of a final day of judgment when Christ returns, at which all those who have refused to repent will be judged (Rev. 20:12–15). Through Christ, believers are not judged according to their own record. They are found to be in Christ, clinging to his righteousness. Unbelievers, however, are found to be sinners. In Revelation 18:1–19:4, John uses the fall of Babylon to point his readers toward further judgment on evil. The passage ends with a song of praise to the Lord on his throne. As the people exult over the downfall of their enemies, they consummate the taunt of Habakkuk 2:6–20.

> **Personal Implications**

Take time to reflect on the implications of Habakkuk 1:12–2:20 for your own life today. Write down your reflections under the three headings we have considered and on the passage as a whole.

1. Gospel Glimpses

2. Whole-Bible Connections

3. Theological Soundings

---

4. Habakkuk 1:12–2:20

> ### As You Finish This Unit . . .

Take a moment now to ask for the Lord's blessing and help as you continue in this study of Lamentations, Habakkuk, and Zephaniah. Take a moment also to look back through this unit of study, to reflect on some key things that the Lord may be teaching you—and perhaps to highlight and underline these things to review again in the future.

Definition

[1] **Righteousness** – The quality of being morally right and without sin. One of God's distinctive attributes. God imputes righteousness to (justifies) those who trust in Jesus Christ.

WEEK 8: WRATH AND MERCY

Habakkuk 3

▲

The Place of the Passage

Habakkuk remembers God's works in history and asks the Lord to reveal his wrath and mercy once again. He prays to the Lord, demonstrating his trust in him through confession of faith. This moves Habakkuk to rejoice in the Lord, for he knows the Lord is his strength (3:18–19).

The Big Picture

Habakkuk looks beyond his immediate circumstances to rejoice in the Lord, who provides strength.

> ### Reflection and Discussion

Read through the complete passage for this study, Habakkuk 3. Then review the questions below concerning this section of Habakkuk and write your notes on them. (For further background, see the *ESV Study Bible*, pages 1853–1855; available online at www.esv.org.)

Habakkuk's Prayer (3:1–19)

Habakkuk's prayer is similar to the psalms of confidence in that he asks for a demonstration of God's wrath and mercy,[1] as he provided in the past. Compare Habakkuk 3:2–3, 9, 13, 19 with Psalms 17 and 90. What terms in Habakkuk's prayer are similar to those in the psalms?

In his prayer, Habakkuk declares that he has heard of the Lord's saving work. How does God deal with his people (v. 2)? Does he issue strict justice according to his people's actions?

What imagery does Habakkuk use to describe God's presence and divine judgment (vv. 3–6)?

Compare 3:16 with 1:2. How has Habakkuk been changed by the Lord's responses to his cries for help?

Does Habakkuk's joy stem from his immediate circumstances (vv. 17–19)? What is the source of his joy?

Read through the following three sections on *Gospel Glimpses, Whole-Bible Connections*, and *Theological Soundings*. Then take time to consider the *Personal Implications* these sections may have for you.

Gospel Glimpses

GOD'S RECORD OF GRACE. Habakkuk's prayer is an example of how God's history of grace informs our vision for the future. By looking back on what God has done in our lives and the lives of his people, we see his character. This strengthens our faith, and we can have confidence that "he who began a good work in you will bring it to completion at the day of Jesus Christ" (Phil. 1:6).

STRENGTH IN THE LORD. When the apostle Paul was suffering greatly, the Lord spoke to him, saying, "My grace is sufficient for you, for my power is made perfect in weakness" (2 Cor. 12:9). When we are weak, then God is strong, for he is our strength (Hab. 3:19; Ps. 18:32, 39). These are important and timely truths for Habakkuk, who experiences the wrath of God through the Lord's chosen instrument, Babylon. Although his immediate circumstances are grave, Habakkuk finds strength in the Lord and rejoices. This ought to direct our attention to the greatest blessing of the gospel. The gospel is not merely concerned with providing benefits to God's people (as glorious as those benefits may be); the gospel is fundamentally about establishing a blessed relationship between God and his people. The good news is not merely that God gives us things but that he gives us the gift of himself.

Whole-Bible Connections

THE GLORY OF THE LORD. God reveals himself throughout Scripture in various ways and forms. Frequently, his presence is accompanied by a vibrant display of light. Habakkuk says, "His splendor covered the heavens, and the earth was full of his praise. His brightness was like the light; rays flashed from his hand; and there he veiled his power" (Hab. 3:3b–4). The tabernacle and temple were special places where God was present with his people. When Moses came down from Sinai after receiving the law, his face shone like the sun. Whenever he would meet with the Lord in the tent of meeting, he would veil his face before the people, presumably in order not to blind them with the glorious light of the Lord reflected in his countenance (Ex. 34:29–35; 2 Cor. 3:7–18). This glory would later be revealed to the people through a new mediator, God incarnate. John speaks of Jesus Christ as a revelation of God's glory: "The Word became flesh and dwelt among us, and we have seen his glory, glory as of the only Son from the Father, full of grace and truth" (John 1:14). The glory of God was revealed through Christ in his transfiguration (Matt. 17:1–13) and especially in his resurrection (Luke 24:36–49; 1 Cor. 15:35–49; Rom. 1:4; Heb. 1:3–4). But in coming days, when the Christ returns, the earth will be filled with the glory of the Lord (Hab. 2:14; compare Rev. 21:22–27).

THE LORD'S VICTORY. Habakkuk declares that the Lord has the victory: "You went out for the salvation of your people, for the salvation of your anointed. You crushed the head of the house of the wicked, laying him bare from thigh to neck" (Hab. 3:13). Jesus is the Lord's anointed (v. 13). He suffered at the hands of wicked men, though he did so willingly (Isa. 53:7; Matt. 26:39; John 10:18). Through Jesus' death and resurrection, the Lord fulfilled the prophecy against the serpent in Genesis 3:15: "I will put enmity between you and the woman, and between your offspring and her offspring; he shall bruise your head, and you shall bruise his heel." In Christ, sin, death, and the Devil will be defeated forever.

Theological Soundings

GOD'S FAITHFULNESS. God is committed to his people. He promises never to leave or forsake them (Deut. 31:6). They may be confident in this fact, because the Lord is who he is. It does not depend on the will of man to keep this commitment. Human beings fail, but God always succeeds (2 Cor. 1:20). While God's people endure suffering and hardship, the Lord is mighty and faithful to save. Jesus spoke of the man who built his house upon the rock: "And the rain fell, and the floods came, and the winds blew and beat on that house, but it did not fall, because it had been founded on the rock. And everyone who hears these words of mine and does not do them will be like a foolish man who built his house on the sand. And the rain fell, and the floods came, and the winds blew and beat against that house, and it fell, and great was the fall of it" (Matt. 7:25–27). Jesus' words are sure and sound. When our lives are built upon him and his precious and great promises (2 Pet. 1:3–4), we can be confident that we will endure any torment of suffering in this life.

PROGRESSIVE REVELATION. God reveals himself to humanity progressively. His revelation is given first in seed form, but throughout the history of salvation[2] it buds and blossoms unto the full flower. In the Old Testament, the Lord reveals himself in types and shadows. But in the New Testament, he reveals himself climactically through his Son, our Savior, Jesus Christ (Heb. 1:1–2). Since "all Scripture is breathed out by God" (2 Tim. 3:16), it is unified and organic (as opposed to artificial). This method of communication emphasizes God's desire to relate to his people. Throughout history, God spoke with his people in varied ages and places as a means of establishing a living bond with them. In Habakkuk, we see God responding to the cries of his people. While they have a limited view, the Lord declares throughout this book that he is already at work to bless them according to his covenant promises.

Personal Implications

Take time to reflect on the implications of Habakkuk 3 for your own life today. Write down your reflections under the three headings we have considered and on the passage as a whole.

1. Gospel Glimpses

2. Whole-Bible Connections

3. Theological Soundings

----

4. Habakkuk 3

> ## As You Finish This Unit . . .

Take a moment now to ask for the Lord's blessing and help as you continue in this study of Lamentations, Habakkuk, and Zephaniah. Take a moment also to look back through this unit of study, to reflect on some key things that the Lord may be teaching you—and perhaps to highlight and underline these things to review again in the future.

Definitions

[1] **Mercy** – Compassion and kindness toward someone experiencing hardship, sometimes even when such suffering results from the person's own sin or foolishness. God displays mercy toward his people and they, in turn, are called to display mercy toward others (Luke 6:36).

[2] **History of salvation** – God's unified plan for all of history, to accomplish the salvation of his people. He accomplished this salvation plan in the work of Jesus Christ on earth, by his life, crucifixion, burial, and resurrection (Eph. 1:3–23). The consummation of God's plan will take place when Jesus Christ comes again to establish the "new heavens and a new earth in which righteousness dwells" (2 Pet. 3:13).

WEEK 9: THE DAY OF THE LORD

Zephaniah 1

▲

Zephaniah was a contemporary of Jeremiah and likely the great-great-grandson of King Hezekiah. His name means "he whom Yahweh hides" or "hidden of Yahweh," which perhaps references the Lord's sheltering his people from his wrath. Zephaniah prophesied during the reign of King Josiah (640–609 BC). Under Manasseh, Josiah's grandfather, Judah had fallen into heinous sin. Yet under Josiah they rediscovered the Book of the Law in 622 BC, and the king brought reform as a result. Most likely, Zephaniah prophesied after this discovery, bringing the message that the Lord was coming in cosmic judgment against the sins of his covenant people as well as against those of the world at large.

The Big Picture

On the day of the Lord, God will come in judgment on both his covenant people and the entire world for their sins.

Reflection and Discussion

Read through the complete passage for this study, Zephaniah 1. Then review the questions below concerning this section of Zephaniah and write your notes on them. (For further background, see the *ESV Study Bible*, pages 1860–1862; available online at www.esv.org.)

1. Judgment Coming against Judah (1:1–6)

The Lord is coming in judgment against all living beings (vv. 2–3) as well as against his covenant people (vv. 4–6). What have they done (vv. 4–6, 12), and what does God's response indicate about his character?

Notice the order of the items listed in Zephaniah 1:2–3. Compare this order with the creation account in Genesis 1:20–26. How does this inform our understanding of God's judgment?

2. The Day of the Lord Is Near (1:7–18)

How many times does Zephaniah use the phrase "the day of the LORD" or similar phrases in this chapter? What is the scope of this "day"? (See notes on Zeph. 1:7–3:20 and Amos 5:18–20 in the *ESV Study Bible*.)

When will the day of the Lord come (v. 14)? How should the people respond to this prophecy?

The people are being judged for their failure to follow the Lord. According to this chapter, where have the people placed their trust instead (vv. 11, 12, 13, 18)? How does the Lord prove superior to these false gods?

Read through the following three sections on *Gospel Glimpses*, *Whole-Bible Connections*, and *Theological Soundings*. Then take time to consider the *Personal Implications* these sections may have for you.

▶ Gospel Glimpses

AN END TO FALSE WORSHIP. The Lord is concerned for the purity of his people. He will rid his holy realm of sin: "I will stretch out my hand against Judah and against all the inhabitants of Jerusalem; and I will cut off from this place the remnant of Baal and the name of the idolatrous priests along with the priests" (Zeph. 1:4). Worship of Baal was practiced in Judah, even being mixed with worship of the Lord. The people would swear to the Lord and then turn around and swear by Milcom (v. 5). They had become syncretists (those who combine multiple religious traditions into one practice), but the Lord will not be placed alongside idols as a spiritual insurance policy. He is coming in judgment to right all wrongs. He is concerned about justice, and the day of the Lord is the great day on which he brings perfect justice to the world. While the day of judgment is terrible, the Lord's grace is evident throughout the rest of Zephaniah's prophecy as he calls his people to repent and find salvation in him.

> ## Whole-Bible Connections

A GREATER JUDGMENT. One day, the Lord will sweep away everything wicked, and nothing will escape his judgment. In Zephaniah 1:2–3, this judgment is described in terms of a de-creation. Notice that the order in which items are listed is the reverse of the order in which they were created: man, beasts, birds, fish. In the days of Noah, the flood was also a form of de-creation. God saw the wickedness of man and that "every intention of the thoughts of his heart was . . . evil continually" (Gen. 6:5). In Noah's day, as well as in Zephaniah's, this resulted in false worship. God responded to the wickedness in Noah's day by bringing the flood against the wicked world. As thorough as the judgment of the flood was, however, the judgment described by Zephaniah would be even more devastating. The language of Zephaniah 1:13–18 is dependent on the covenant curses described in Deuteronomy (Deut. 4:11; 28:29, 30, 39; 32:21–22). The prophet is delivering the Lord's word. Specifically, he is prosecuting a case by bringing to bear the terms of a covenant lawsuit. Zephaniah's prophecy refers to a judgment to come in the relative near-term of his day, but also to the final judgment at the end of days. That judgment will be complete and final.

GODLY ATTIRE. The Lord calls everyone to a banquet: "Be silent before the Lord GOD! For the day of the LORD is near; the LORD has prepared a sacrifice and consecrated his guests" (v. 7). Although this is a banquet, it is not a celebration for the guests. Instead, the people are being judged for their idolatry. On this day, the Lord will punish the officials and the king's sons for wearing "foreign attire" (v. 8). These people were probably wearing special garments for pagan rituals (see 2 Kings 10:22); they do not belong in God's house among God's people. In Scripture, clothing can be used to demonstrate identity and membership in a community. Jesus spoke of this dynamic in Matthew 22:11–13, describing a king's coming into his banquet only to see a man with no wedding garment. When the man cannot account for his lack of appropriate attire, he is cast into the outer darkness: "In that place there will be weeping and gnashing of teeth" (v. 13). Paul calls people to put off the old self, which is identified with the world and its sinful way of life, and to put on the new self in Christ (Eph. 4:22–24), dressed in his righteousness (Rom. 13:14).

SPARED FROM JUDGMENT. Zephaniah proclaimed the day of the Lord, and such a day came. The Lord poured out his wrath on Judah when the Babylonians destroyed Jerusalem and took them into exile. But as noted earlier, the great and final day of wrath is yet to come, the day on which the fullness of God's wrath will come upon the entire world (Rom. 2:5; Rev. 6:16–17). The apostle Paul proclaimed this message to the philosophers in Athens (Acts 17:30–31). God in his grace has overlooked past times of ignorance, but now he commands everyone to repent of their sins. To escape the judgment to come, we must be found *in Christ*, because he alone can save. The prophet Joel also spoke of the final judgment on the day of the Lord, and the apostle Peter invoked that prophecy in his sermon at Pentecost (Acts 2:17–21). Even on the great and terrible day of the Lord, "Everyone who calls on the name of the LORD shall be saved" (Joel 2:32). This prophecy teaches us what Christ must suffer in order to accomplish salvation for his people. The Gospels tell us that Jesus' crucifixion was accompanied by earthquakes, resurrections, darkness, and covenant curses (Matt. 27:45, 51–53; 28:2; Mark 15:33; Luke 23:44). Those found in Christ have escaped final judgment because that judgment came upon Jesus in his death.

Theological Soundings

COVENANT. God promises to bless[1] his people within a context of commitment and instruction. This is the only antidote to people wandering away from the truths of God, as seen in the people of Zephaniah's day. Such a relationship of commitment to God was formalized when the Lord sovereignly established a covenant with his people that included continuing terms and obligations. He established blessings for obedience and curses (or punishments) for disobedience, and the Lord pledged to lead and guide his people and summon them to love and faithfulness. The covenant relationship came to its greatest expression in the new covenant, mediated by Jesus Christ and established in his blood (Heb. 9:11–28). He bore the covenantal curse that we deserve, and we receive the blessings he has secured through his obedience and sacrifice.

DIVINE JUSTICE. The people of God transgressed the covenant, as made clear by Zephaniah's scathing rebuke of their conduct. God established curses for such unfaithfulness within the terms of the covenant, and he must abide by his word. He cannot lie (Titus 1:2); he is truth, and in him there is no darkness at all (1 John 1:5). According to God's unchanging character, he must punish sin. The gospel points us to Jesus Christ, who fulfills the obligations of the covenant. He establishes a new covenant in his own blood and gives to his people a perfect obedience (Heb. 5:8). Divine justice is satisfied in Christ, and his people receive the covenantal blessings he secured. Yet those who reject Christ and his offer of salvation will receive the just deserts for their sin: an eternity of conscious torment in hell.

Personal Implications

Take time to reflect on the implications of Zephaniah 1 for your own life today. Write down your reflections under the three headings we have considered and on the passage as a whole.

1. Gospel Glimpses

2. Whole-Bible Connections

3. Theological Soundings

4. Zephaniah 1

As You Finish This Unit . . .

Take a moment now to ask for the Lord's blessing and help as you continue in this study of Lamentations, Habakkuk, and Zephaniah. Take a moment also to look back through this unit of study, to reflect on some key things that the Lord may be teaching you—and perhaps to highlight and underline these things to review again in the future.

Definition

[1] **Bless** – To worship or praise another, especially God; to bestow goodness on another.

Week 10: Pride
before the Fall

Zephaniah 2

The Place of the Passage

The people's pride has blinded them to the coming disaster, but the prophet Zephaniah makes clear that God will judge both his people and their enemies for their sins. Notwithstanding, God calls his people to repent, for he will preserve a remnant.[1]

The Big Picture

Though all have sinned against the Lord and deserve his wrath, repentance[2] is still possible.

Reflection and Discussion

Read through the complete passage for this study, Zephaniah 2. Then review the questions concerning this section of Zephaniah and write your notes on them. (For further background, see the *ESV Study Bible*, pages 1862–1864; available online at www.esv.org.)

1. Repentance Is Still Possible (2:1–3)

God is bringing judgment against the proud people of the nations, yet there is still time for Judah to repent. Whom, specifically, does the Lord address in verse 3?

What does the Lord call the people of Judah to do (v. 3)? Is this something the people could do in pride?

2. The Nations Are Warned (2:4–15)

What specific sins does Zephaniah mention for each nation? What do these sins indicate about a proper approach to God?

What does the geography of Judah's neighbors indicate about the scope of God's judgment?

Read through the following three sections on *Gospel Glimpses, Whole-Bible Connections*, and *Theological Soundings*. Then take time to consider the *Personal Implications* these sections may have for you.

Gospel Glimpses

INESCAPABLE JUDGMENT. In Zephaniah 1, the Lord had declared that he would sweep away everything wicked. Judah had fallen into great sin, and the Lord sent his prophet to remind his people of the covenant curses. The nations surrounding Judah had a front-row seat to the work of the Lord. They would see the judgment God would bring upon his own people. Here he calls his people to action: gather together and seek the Lord (2:1, 3). The day of the Lord will come, and judgment will come upon their neighbors on all sides. Philistia is mentioned first (2:4–7). They were to the west of Judah, near the sea. Moab and Ammon were to the northeast of Judah; their taunts and insults are emphasized in verses 8 and 10. The Lord himself has taken offense at this, since Judah is his covenant people. The remnant of God's people will plunder them; God's people will enjoy their wealth. Cush was to the south of Judah. Then comes Assyria to the north; she is judged for her pride (v. 15).

PRESERVING A REMNANT. God's grace is revealed in his preservation of a remnant (vv. 6, 7, 9). After the Lord judges, only a few survivors will be left. These are not the proud, but the ones he has preserved in humility. The presence of a remnant demonstrates that God will not destroy his covenant people. He has not forgotten them nor left them to languish; he will restore their fortunes. Shepherds and their folds will return to the land (compare Ps. 23:1–3).

Whole-Bible Connections

SODOM AND GOMORRAH. Moab and Ammon are mentioned in Zephaniah 2:8. They were blood relatives of Israel because they were the descendants of Lot's daughters, who made their father drunk and then lay with him. Moab and Ammon were incestuously conceived just after the destruction of Sodom and Gomorrah (Gen. 19:23–38). This beginning led to a tumultuous history with God's people, as Moab and Ammon oppressed and attacked Judah throughout the years. Their judgment is linked to the judgment that came upon those ancient cities in Genesis 19, and in the end, Moab and Ammon shall become like Sodom and Gomorrah. While they at one time were like a green and fruitful land, they would now bear nettles, salt pits, and eternal waste (Zeph. 2:9). Their judgment calls to mind the effects of the curse on Adam after he fell into sin:

"Cursed is the ground because of you; in pain you shall eat of it all the days of your life; thorns and thistles it shall bring forth for you; and you shall eat the plants of the field. By the sweat of your face you shall eat bread, till you return to the ground, for out of it you were taken; for you are dust, and to dust you shall return" (Gen. 3:17–19). Apart from Christ, we, like Sodom, are cursed and will receive the full wrath of God. With that future in mind, Jesus declared that the cities who rejected his disciples would receive an even greater judgment than that of Sodom and Gomorrah (Matt. 10:5–15; Luke 10:1–12). When Jesus returns on the final day of judgment, the wicked will experience his wrath (Luke 17:20–37).

PRIDE BEFORE THE FALL. Assyria is the most blatant example of pride in this passage, but she is just one instance of a recurring theme in Scripture. Consider the people of Babel, who built a tower to reach into the heavens (Gen. 11:1–9); or Nebuchadnezzar, who raised himself above God in Daniel 4:30: "Is not this great Babylon, which I have built by my mighty power as a royal residence and for the glory of my majesty?" God humiliated every one of these pretenders to his throne. If the nations will not repent, they will be humiliated as well (Zeph. 2:11). The pattern of life for the nations is earthly glory leading to eternal shame. The pattern of life for Christ and his people is earthly suffering leading to eternal and heavenly glory (Phil. 2:5–11). Consequently, Christians must have the patience and humility not to act out in revenge. Vengeance is the Lord's; he will repay (Deut. 32:35; Rom. 12:19). God always confronts sin; he is holy[3] and just, and sin cannot stand. Verses 7–9 of Zephaniah 2 describe how the Lord will hand over the lands of the nations to be the possession of his covenant people. Indeed, the meek shall inherit the earth (Matt. 5:5).

▶ Theological Soundings

REPENTANCE UNTO LIFE. In order to escape the wrath and curse of God due to us for sin, as described in Zephaniah 2, God requires faith in his Messiah, Jesus Christ, and repentance. Repentance is not merely feeling sorry for sin. Neither is it regret over the consequences of wrongdoing. True repentance involves self-examination, sorrow over sin, and turning away from such sin. The Holy Spirit works the grace of repentance in the life of the sinner so that he or she understands the danger and filthiness of sin while also apprehending God's mercy in Christ. The sinner grieves for and hates sin, turns to God for forgiveness, and strives toward new obedience in Christ. Such a person can be fully confident that he or she has been saved completely by God from the wrath to come.

VISIBLE AND INVISIBLE CHURCH. God has chosen a specific people to save. This is not based on anything good within themselves. Rather, God *elects* them. But it is important to note that there are different types of election[4] that come to bear on this passage in Zephaniah. For example, the nation of Israel was elected or chosen by God, but "not all who are descended from Israel belong to Israel" (Rom. 9:6). While the nation was elected corporately, not everyone was elected individually. Likewise, theologians often make a distinction between "formal" and "vital" union with Christ. While many may be identified outwardly with God's people, some of these people refuse to repent and believe in Jesus Christ. These individuals are not vitally united to him; they do not abide in him (John 15:1–11). Paul describes this in Romans 11. Those who do not believe will be "cut off," whereas those who repent and believe may even be grafted back in. To understand how the covenant people may be a mixture of believers and unbelievers, theologians speak of the "visible" and "invisible" church. While various Christian traditions differ on the finer points of ecclesiology, the visible church includes those who have received the outward sign of baptism and belong to a local congregation, whereas the invisible church comprises only the elect, those whose names are written in the Lamb's book of life (Rev. 3:5; 13:8; 17:8; 21:27).

Personal Implications

Take time to reflect on the implications of Zephaniah 2 for your own life today. Write down your reflections under the three headings we have considered and on the passage as a whole.

1. Gospel Glimpses

2. Whole-Bible Connections

3. Theological Soundings

4. Zephaniah 2

> ## As You Finish This Unit . . .

Take a moment now to ask for the Lord's blessing and help as you continue in this study of Lamentations, Habakkuk, and Zephaniah. Take a moment also to look back through this unit of study, to reflect on some key things that the Lord may be teaching you—and perhaps to highlight and underline these things to review again in the future.

Definitions

[1] **Remnant** – In the Bible, a portion of people who remain after most others are destroyed by some catastrophe. The notion of a remnant can be found in various events recorded in Scripture, including the flood (Genesis 6–8) and the return of exiled Judah (Ezra 9).

[2] **Repentance** – A complete change of heart and mind regarding one's overall attitude toward God or one's individual actions. True regeneration and conversion are always accompanied by repentance.

[3] **Holiness** – A quality possessed by something or someone set apart for special use. When applied to God, it refers to his utter perfection and complete transcendence over creation. God's people are called to imitate his holiness (Lev. 19:2), which means being set apart from sin and reserved for his purposes.

[4] **Election** – In theology, God's sovereign choice of people for redemption and eternal life. Also referred to as "predestination."

WEEK 11: THE LORD REJOICES

Zephaniah 3

▲

In Zephaniah 2, judgment was pronounced upon Judah's neighbors on all sides. In this chapter, we learn that Judah's behavior was not that different from the behavior of her pagan neighbors. The city of Jerusalem has proven recalcitrant (3:2). She does not listen and will receive no correction. The people neither trust nor draw near to the Lord. This is a failure of all aspects of society, for the prophets, priests, and kings are not carrying out their most important work. But the Lord has promised to purify the people and call to himself distant ones from the nations. He will rejoice over his people and exult over them with loud singing (3:17).

The Big Picture

God demonstrates his grace in restoring his people and calling the nations to himself.

Reflection and Discussion

Read through the complete passage for this study, Zephaniah 3. Then review the questions below concerning this section of Zephaniah and write your notes on them. (For further background, see the *ESV Study Bible*, pages 1864–1867; available online at www.esv.org.)

1. Judgment and Conversion (3:1–13)

How is the city of Jerusalem described? What has become of her rulers, prophets, and priests (vv. 3–4)?

What does God call the city to do (vv. 7–8)?

What must be done for Judah to return to the Lord (vv. 11–13)?

2. Israel's Joy and Restoration (3:14–20)

What does it mean for Judah to have the king in her midst (v. 15)?

The Lord is the ultimate singer of this prophecy (v. 17). How is this related to the joy of God's people?

Read through the following three sections on *Gospel Glimpses*, *Whole-Bible Connections*, and *Theological Soundings*. Then take time to consider the *Personal Implications* these sections may have for you.

Gospel Glimpses

BLESSING TO THE FAMILIES OF THE EARTH. Although Zephaniah has declared that judgment will come upon the nations, there is still hope, for God will bring the nations to himself. This truth can be seen throughout the Old Testament. For example, Abraham was the father of the nation even though he was a pagan. God called him (when he was still Abram) out of Haran. Rahab, a Canaanite prostitute, helped the Israelite spies and was protected under God's covenantal care. Ruth, a Moabite, was another stranger to the Lord's covenant. After her Israelite husband died, Ruth remained with her mother-in-law and came to live among God's people, rather than returning to Moab. She believed in Yahweh and was brought into his covenant. Both Rahab and Ruth were included in Jesus' genealogy. This is also the testimony of the New Testament, which declares that the Gentiles are included in the people of God (Ephesians 1–2; Gal. 3:28). Pentecost was a fulfillment of Joel's prophecy regarding the day of the Lord (Acts 2:16–21) as well as an example of the Lord purifying the nation's speech (Zeph. 3:9). At Pentecost, the people of God understood the apostles in their own languages (Acts 2:1–13). This was a reversal of the curse that God had set upon the people of Babel in response to their autonomy and pride (Gen. 11:1–9). While this blessing of the Holy Spirit came first upon the Jews, the Spirit later came upon the Gentiles as well (Acts 10:44–46). This underscores God's grace, because our ethnic heritage, genealogy, or geographic location does not dictate our inclusion in or exclusion from the covenant (Gal. 3:26–29). All types of people are saved by God.

A GREATER PARADISE. God will change our shame into praise and renown in all the earth (Zeph. 3:19). In fact, the nations will stream to the Lord, who will reign from Mount Zion (Isa. 2:2–4; Mic. 4:1–5). God will restore the fortunes of his people. As Christians, we are not looking to go back to Eden. We do not want paradise merely restored; we long for paradise consummated.[1] This is precisely what Jesus Christ does in bringing his people to the new heavens and new earth (Isa. 65:17–25). The Lord will dwell among us perpetually. He overcomes our fear, sadness, guilt, grief, and anxiety (Zeph. 3:17). His people will be confirmed in true knowledge, righteousness, and holiness, and will be established forever in glory (Eph. 4:24; 1 Cor. 15:50–52; 1 John 3:1–2). This is the beauty of Zephaniah that shines through the devastation of final judgment.

Whole-Bible Connections

THE JUDGMENT TO COME. The prophecies of Zephaniah were delivered to the Jews during the reign of Josiah. The promised judgment would come upon Judah in 587 BC. It came again in AD 70 when Jerusalem was attacked and the temple destroyed. While the prophecies delivered through Zephaniah have reference to both of these historical events, the prophet introduces a judgment that expands to include the entire world (3:8, 10). This is the final judgment still to come. It brings into view the judgment of Noah's day, when God judged the entire world for sin (Gen. 6:17–18). The Lord promised never again to destroy the world by water, but a judgment is coming in which the earth will be destroyed by fire (Malachi 3–4; Matt. 24:3–44; 2 Pet. 3:10).

CHRIST THE KING. When Israel sought a king like those of the other nations, a king who turned out to be Saul, they were also rejecting the Lord as King. But when David, a man after God's own heart, ascended to the throne, the Lord established his throne forever (2 Sam. 7:16). Nevertheless, there were many years of failed monarchies in Israel and Judah. Zephaniah prophesied during the reign of Josiah, who brought reforms. But remarkably, his successors still fell short in disobedience. The last king of Judah was Zedekiah, a sort of puppet king installed by Nebuchadnezzar II of Babylon. And yet the throne of Judah and David would not remain unoccupied. It is occupied now by the greater David, Jesus Christ (Acts 2:29–36). Today the Lord blesses his people through their King, Jesus Christ, who reigns and rules over his people and defends them from their enemies. All the shadows and types of the Old Testament converge in the person and work of Jesus.

Theological Soundings

THE UNIVERSAL OFFER OF SALVATION. God does not take pleasure in the destruction of the wicked (see 2 Pet. 3:9). Rather, he rejoices over those who repent and seek refuge in him. He commands all people everywhere to repent (Acts 17:30), promising salvation to those who call upon the name of the Lord Jesus (Joel 2:28–32; Acts 2:17–21).

SALVATION BY GRACE. This passage makes clear that God is the one who saves (Zeph. 3:17). Salvation is based not on works[2] of the law or human merit but on God's grace (Rom. 4:1–5; 9:16; Gal. 2:15–16; Titus 3:4–6). Clearly, mankind has not merited salvation. All humans have transgressed the law of the Lord and deserve his wrath and curse. Despite this, God saves those who look to him in faith and repentance.

SINGING IN WORSHIP. In response to God's great acts of salvation, we are called to praise his name in worship. God liberates his people from the captivity of sin, which drives them to rejoice. It is fitting that we would worship by singing. The apostle Paul exhorts the Colossians, "Let the word of Christ dwell in you richly, teaching and admonishing one another in all wisdom, singing psalms and hymns and spiritual songs, with thankfulness in your hearts to God" (Col. 3:16). This is a biblical pattern that directs our lives. When God speaks and acts, his people are moved (see, e.g., Psalms 95; 96; 147). This worshipful capacity is a privilege given to human beings, and it is directed and informed by God's person and work. His singing in Zephaniah demonstrates that our singing expresses his image in us, and even Christ himself joins us in our midst as we sing (Heb. 2:12).

Personal Implications

Take time to reflect on the implications of Zephaniah 3 for your own life today. Write down your reflections under the three headings we have considered and on the passage as a whole.

1. Gospel Glimpses

2. Whole-Bible Connections

3. Theological Soundings

4. Zephaniah 3

As You Finish This Unit . . .

Take a moment now to ask for the Lord's blessing and help as you continue in this study of Lamentations, Habakkuk, and Zephaniah. Take a moment also to look back through this unit of study, to reflect on some key things that the Lord may be teaching you—and perhaps to highlight and underline these things to review again in the future.

Definitions

[1] **Consummation** – In Christian theology, the final and full establishment of the kingdom of God, when the heavens and earth will be made new and God will rule over all things forever (2 Pet. 3:13; Revelation 11; 19–22).

[2] **Works** – Actions and attitudes, either good or bad. True faith in Christ will inevitably produce good works that are pleasing to God.

Week 12: Summary and Conclusion

▲

The Big Picture

Whether warning of coming judgment or lamenting its realization, the books of Lamentations, Habakkuk, and Zephaniah wrestle with the reality of sin and its consequences. God's people broke his covenant. They transgressed his law and thus must experience his wrath. Sin is a universal reality, and the truths in these books regarding sin's reality and its consequences apply today as much as they did when they were first uttered. Because God's justice must be satisfied, he sent his Son, Jesus Christ, to save his people from the wrath to come. Lamentations, Habakkuk, and Zephaniah express the pain and suffering of God's people as they live in a fallen world while also directing their gaze toward the blessed hope of salvation in Jesus Christ.

Gospel Glimpses

These prophets minister in dark times and wrestle with crippling questions. They are driven to ask how long it will take for the Lord to deliver his people. They struggle to understand how a righteous God could use a nation more wicked than they to judge them. These are questions prompted even today as the church suffers in this sin-cursed world. But the overwhelming message of

Lamentations, Habakkuk, and Zephaniah is "strength for today and bright hope for tomorrow," as Thomas O. Chisholm wrote in the hymn "Great Is Thy Faithfulness," based loosely on Lamentations 3:22–23. The Lord triumphs over sin through the truly faithful one, Jesus Christ.

Have Lamentations, Habakkuk, and Zephaniah brought new clarity to your understanding of the gospel? How so?

Were there any particular passages or themes in these books that led you to a fresh understanding and grasp of God's grace to us through Jesus?

Whole-Bible Connections

Israel was chosen and set apart as a holy nation unto the Lord (Ex. 19:5–6; 1 Pet. 2:9–10), who set his love upon them and called them out of Egypt. He protected and led them through the wilderness into the Promised Land. Though God was faithful to his covenant, the people were not. They rejected him, and the Lord sent his wrath, removing the people from the land of blessing and into exile at the hands of Assyria and Babylon. The history of God's dealings with Israel is part of a larger lesson about our bondage to sin and our need of salvation in Jesus Christ. Man is born into a state of sin and misery, yet God has sent his Son, Jesus Christ, to take our place. Jesus recapitulated the history of Israel (see Matthew 1–4), though he succeeded in every way. As the truly obedient Son, Christ reversed the curse by bearing the sin of his people, suffering the full wrath of God in their place, and covering them with his perfect righteousness. In Christ, we find a restoration greater than any return to Old Testament Canaan—the promise of dwelling with the triune God in the new heavens and the new earth (Ps. 84:10; Isa. 65:17–25; Hebrews 3–4; 11–12; Rev. 22:1–5).

How has this study increased your understanding of the biblical storyline of redemption?

Were there any themes emphasized in Lamentations, Habakkuk, or Zephaniah that help you to deepen your grasp of the Bible's unity?

Have any passages or themes expanded your understanding of the redemption that Jesus provides, which he began at his first coming and will consummate at his return?

What connections between Lamentations, Habakkuk, Zephaniah, and the New Testament were new to you?

Theological Soundings

Habakkuk, Lamentations, and Zephaniah contribute much to Christian theology. They set forth doctrines such as God's justice and wrath, which are revealed on the "day of the Lord," while also demonstrating God's steadfast love and mercy given to his people in the forgiveness of sins through his Son, Jesus Christ.

Has your theology shifted in minor or major ways during the course of studying Lamentations, Habakkuk, and Zephaniah? How so?

Has your understanding of the nature and character of God been deepened throughout this study? How so?

What unique contributions do Lamentations, Habakkuk, and Zephaniah make toward your understanding of who Jesus is and what he accomplished through his life, death, and resurrection?

What, specifically, do Lamentations, Habakkuk, and Zephaniah teach us about the human condition and our need of redemption?

Personal Implications

God wrote the books of Lamentations, Habakkuk, and Zephaniah to transform us. As you reflect on them as a whole, what implications do you see for your life?

What implications for life flow from your reflections on the questions already asked in this week's study concerning Gospel Glimpses, Whole-Bible Connections, and Theological Soundings?

What have you learned in Lamentations, Habakkuk, and Zephaniah that might lead you to praise God, turn away from sin, or trust more firmly in his promises?

> As You Finish Studying Lamentations, Habakkuk, and Zephaniah . . .

We rejoice with you as you finish studying the books of Lamentations, Habakkuk, and Zephaniah! May this study become part of your Christian walk of faith, day by day and week by week throughout all your life. Now we would greatly encourage you to study the Word of God on a week-by-week basis. To continue your study of the Bible, we would encourage you to consider other books in the *Knowing the Bible* series, and to visit www.knowingthebibleseries.org.

Lastly, take a moment to look back through this study. Review the notes you have written, and the things you have highlighted or underlined. Reflect again on the key themes that the Lord has been teaching you about himself and about his Word. May these things become a treasure for you throughout your life—this we pray in the name of the Father, and the Son, and the Holy Spirit. Amen.

KNOWING THE BIBLE STUDY GUIDE SERIES

Experience the *Grace* of God in the *Word* of God, Book by Book

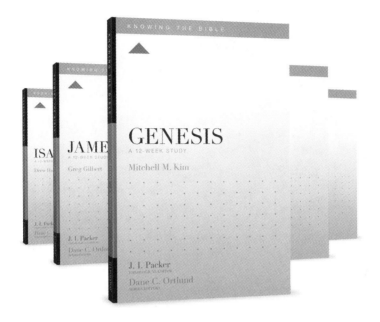

Series Volumes

- Genesis
- Exodus
- Leviticus
- Numbers
- Deuteronomy
- Joshua
- Judges
- Ruth and Esther
- 1–2 Samuel
- 1–2 Kings
- 1–2 Chronicles
- Ezra and Nehemiah
- Job
- Psalms
- Proverbs
- Ecclesiastes
- Song of Solomon

- Isaiah
- Jeremiah
- Lamentations, Habakkuk, and Zephaniah
- Ezekiel
- Daniel
- Hosea
- Joel, Amos, and Obadiah
- Jonah, Micah, and Nahum
- Haggai, Zechariah, and Malachi
- Matthew
- Mark
- Luke

- John
- Acts
- Romans
- 1 Corinthians
- 2 Corinthians
- Galatians
- Ephesians
- Philippians
- Colossians and Philemon
- 1–2 Thessalonians
- 1–2 Timothy and Titus
- Hebrews
- James
- 1–2 Peter and Jude
- 1–3 John
- Revelation

crossway.org/knowingthebible